Seeing Yourself
in the Mirror of
Truth

To: Lori

May the light of His
Truth reveal how truly
beautiful you are in
Jesus Christ.

Laura Shout

Seeing Yourself
in the Mirror of
Truth

Freedom from a Distorted Self Image

Laura
Shoemaker

WinePressPublishing
Great Books, Defined.

WinePress Publishing (PO Box 428, Enumclaw, WA 98022) functions only as book publisher. As such, the ultimate design, content, editorial accuracy, and views expressed or implied in this work are those of the author.

All Scripture quotations, unless otherwise indicated, are taken from the *Holy Bible, New International Version®, NIV®*. Copyright © 1973, 1978, 1984 by Biblica, Inc.™ Used by permission of Zondervan. All rights reserved worldwide. www.zondervan.com

Scripture quotations marked AMP are taken from *The Amplified Bible*, Copyright 1954, 1958, 1962, 1964, 1965, 1987 by The Zondervan Corporation and The Lockman Foundation.

ISBN 13: 978-1-4141-1969-4
ISBN 10: 1-4141-1969-0
Library of Congress Catalog Card Number: 2010939672

This book is dedicated to those God surrounded me
with as I battled to find my freedom in Jesus Christ:

To my parents, Ken and Brenda Baker,
who never looked back in giving me life
and who loved me unconditionally.

To my husband, Jon Shoemaker,
who provided me the love and
environment I needed to be healed.

To my mentor and friend, Kim Lambert,
who passionately taught me how
to run hard after Jesus.

Contents

Introduction

A MIRROR CAN be a friend and an enemy. While mirrors come in handy when we're putting on makeup and getting our hair just right, they also reveal flaws we'd rather forget about or didn't know were there. Often we have other "mirrors" in our lives as well, such as the opinions of others, social expectations, and deep-rooted insecurities. As many have discovered, these mirrors are never helpful. They fill our heads with lies, perpetuating fears and feelings of inferiority. It leaves us wondering: is it possible to find a mirror that tells the truth and leaves us feeling beautiful rather than ugly? The answer is "yes"! I, like many others, have found such a mirror—the mirror of God's Word.

When we learn how to partner with God through His Word, allowing Him to uncover the lies as we discover His truth, He begins to tame, shape, and polish our whole image—inside and out. Learning how to cooperate with God is crucial in finding our own true beauty. Once we begin to see and understand the truth about ourselves, we begin to know and live as the person we were created to be. And that, my friend, is where you find the freedom to live the life God has for you.

From personal experience, I know what it looks like to live in the reflected ugliness of fear, doubt, self-condemnation, perfectionism, guilt, and anxiety. But I also know what it looks like to be transformed and take on the beauty of Jesus Christ. I was extremely held captive by lies until I started learning and living God's Word. It is His truth that sets us free; and until we begin to know it, we can't begin to live it.

I have written this book not only in the light of my transformation, but also in the light of His Word. Reading, absorbing, understanding, believing, and living His Word is the only mirror that will make you beautiful. Throughout this book, you will see and read a lot of Scripture. This is the mirror I want you to focus on. The rest of the book is just to help you understand these verses, but the real power is in His Word. I highly encourage you to prayerfully read each verse not only with your eyes and mind, but also with your heart and soul. May His beauty astonish you and transform you into the beautiful person He has always intended for you to be.

CHAPTER 1

The Journey to Truth

If you hold to my teachings, you are really my disciples. Then you will know the truth, and the truth will set you free.

—Jesus Christ,
according to the gospel of John 8:31–32

A S A LITTLE girl, I would often look in the mirror after getting in trouble and tell myself, "Bad La Me!" ("Bad Laura Marie!"). I remember angrily pointing and shaking my finger at the reflection staring back at me while I voiced my disappointment to the little girl in the mirror. I obviously took my discipline very seriously, but in reality, I hated disappointing those I wanted to please, and I fussed at myself when I did. It is funny to think back on this childhood memory, but at the time, my disappointing correction was more serious than I realized: I unknowingly exchanged the truth of healthy discipline for a lie of condemnation.

Years of continual condemnation viciously followed me while I was growing up, and I deliberately blamed

1

myself for every disappointment. Instead of looking at disappointments and uncertainties as opportunities to grow, I exchanged the truth of Christ's forgiveness and His perfection for a lie of condemnation and self-perfection. For me, it wasn't enough to learn from my parents' discipline or from my mistakes. I had to find someone to blame for my imperfections, and I usually blamed myself. Because of this, I became a slave to my own goodness and relied on others to validate my worth.

It wasn't until I was thirty-one years old that I began to see the truthful perspective of what I really looked like. As my own mirrors were replaced with God's one true mirror, I started to see the reality of all the lies that had distorted and disfigured my image for so long. One by one, those lies were revealed to me, and I learned how to humbly give each one to the cross. Then and only then did I begin to see myself as God intended me to—beautiful in Jesus Christ.

Influences that Shape Us

Just like a ball of clay in the hands of a sculptor, all of us are easily shaped and molded by what we allow to influence us. Sculpting tools abound in our world of many influences; we can continually be shaped by thoughts, feelings, family, our spouse, friends, teachers, co-workers, media, movie stars, government, culture, religion, experiences, insecurities, and even our own hurts. In my earlier example, I let my condemning thoughts mold me into a girl who could never be good enough.

Our images are so fragile. Instead of looking at ourselves in the mirror truthfully, many of us cloud our vision with lies. We let people and the world shape our thoughts, which then distorts and confuses the way we view ourselves. So instead of being molded by God's truth of grace, humility, confidence, and Christ's forgiveness, our thoughts and vision have been distorted by the lies of worry, condemnation, insecurity, fear, perfectionism, self-reliance, doubt, and pride (just to name a few).

As our Creator, God knew we needed a standard of truth to live by. He was not about to leave us alone to figure life out on our own. God has given us a mirror (an absolute standard of truth) that we can look to and live by so we can lead fulfilling and fruitful lives. God has made Himself available to us so we can see and know ourselves in the light of His truth.

Knowing what God says to be true is like having a lie detector planted in our minds. When a lie comes our way, we are able to recognize it because we know what the truth is. His truth lets us know what to believe and what not to believe—what will harm us and what will protect us.

As individuals, we can't force others to agree with or go along with what we believe to be true—just like I can't force you to believe the words in this book. We can only look to ourselves and decide if what we believe is based on what God says to be true or not. This is where it all starts—with you and with me. If we can't change as individuals, our families can't change. And if our families can't change, then our communities can't change. And if our communities can't change, our countries and world can't change. So I have to ask: Have you thought about what you believe? Or better yet, have you thought about what mirror you are looking into? Are you ready to see yourself in the mirror of truth?

Lost?

Getting lost is not something most of us have on our "bucket lists." We don't intentionally wake up each morning and say, "I want to lose my way today." In fact, most of us become really frustrated when we don't know where we are going. Whether we are driving to visit family or going through a hard time in a relationship, being lost or confused is not a fun thing. It makes us feel helpless, hopeless, and inadequate—not a good way to spend our time. However, there are many people today who have been misplaced and don't even know it (I was one of those people). There are also some who suspect they are lost but don't even bother to stop and seek out the right direction. They continue waddling on the wrong road, trying to ignore the fact that they have been misguided. Irrespective of the reason, being lost is not where God wants us. He wants us to be found. Matthew 18:12–14 teaches us about this:

> If a man owns a hundred sheep, and one of them wanders away, will he not leave the ninety-nine on the hills and go to look for the one that wandered off? And if he finds it, I tell you the truth, he is happier about that one sheep than about the ninety-nine that did not wander off. In the same way your Father in heaven is not willing that any of these little ones should be lost.

Imagine what would happen if seven of your eight children loved and obeyed you the best they could, but the eighth child ignorantly wandered off into disobedience and rebellion. Would you not worry about the eighth child since you already had seven who loved and obeyed you? Would you just ignore your lost child? No, you would mourn over your lost child. You would pray for your lost sheep to be found so he or she could be under the protective care of your love. God is like that when it comes to us. In fact, the heavens rejoice over one lost sinner who repents more than over ninety-nine persons who have already found righteousness (Luke 15:7).

Even though it is not God's will for us to be lost, just like it is not a parent's will for his or her child to be lost, we often are lost because of our own ignorance and child-like rebellion. It takes God's intervention to draw us back to Himself, and it takes a surrendered willingness on our part to receive His guided help.

Being lost reminds me of a trip we took last year to Dallas, Texas. Our primary purpose in Dallas was to attend my son's baseball tournament, but we were also hoping for an opportunity to see my aunt Larue, who wasn't far from where he was playing.

As it turned out, we did get some time between games, but our visit had to be quick since we only had two hours until the next game started. So we piled into our Ford Expedition, drove to McDonalds® to grab a bite to eat, and quickly headed to our destination.

I was excited that my great aunt, who was eighty-one at the time, would get to see her nephews (it had been five years since she last saw them). Even though she lived out of town, my boys knew of Aunt Larue from the many birthday cards she had sent them. I really wanted to make the most of our time with her and hoped our visit would last longer than our time in the car.

Already fixated on the amount of time we were spending on the road, I realized something was wrong when our drive stretched from thirty minutes to forty-five. By the time we discovered we were going the wrong way, we were already way behind schedule.

Much to my dismay, I'd read the map incorrectly. (I have never been good with directions, even with a map). So my husband, Jon, pulled the car onto the side of the road, grabbed the map from my hand, and figured out where I went wrong in the navigating process.

As we turned back around, I knew we would not have time to visit my aunt. Justin had to be back for his next game, and we'd taken way too much time driving in the wrong direction.

At this point, I started crying. Not only did I feel like a fool for reading the map incorrectly, but also I'd messed up our plans to see aunt Larue. I felt absolutely horrible.

We eventually dropped Justin off just in time for his next game, and then the rest of us hit the road for a second time to visit aunt Larue. Even though we missed Justin's game and my aunt didn't get to see both of her nephews, we were grateful for the time the three of us got to spend with her.

How many times do we do this on our journey through life? We wander down a road, not even realizing we are headed in the wrong direction. We either drive too far in our own strength, missing the turn we needed to take, or we unknowingly exhaust ourselves by going around and around in circles.

Inevitably, when we are on a wrong path, our ignorance will bring us to a point where we don't know what to do or where to go. Sometimes we even feel so lost that we end up staying stuck on the side of the road and settle into a "getting nowhere" routine that God never intended for us to have. And then there are those who choose not to find the right way at all and end up going down a path that ends in eternal destruction.

But let me tell you, my friend, as long as you are on this side of eternity, there is hope to be found, and there is definitely a true and right way for you to go. As you will discover throughout this book, not only can you get back on the right path, but also your time spent wandering can be restored and multiplied—just like my visit with aunt Larue. Our time together may not have been my idea of a perfect visit, but it was a longer visit than it would have been if we had made it there the first time we tried.

On my own road of life, I have come across a handful of discouraging bumps and confusing, sharp turns. But it wasn't until I reached a breaking point that I definitely knew something wasn't right.

In the summer of 2003, we had just moved back from living in Singapore. I returned to the United States with our two boys while Jon finished his work overseas. Justin and Brandon were six and three years old at the time. When I arrived in Houston after a twenty-four-hour plane ride with our boys by my side, I was exhausted. But my gas-burning journey had just begun.

In the fall of 2000, before we moved, we sold our house and our cars and put the majority of our household belongings in storage. So when I moved back, it was up to me to find a car and a house and get everything unpacked and hooked up so we could be settled before school started that fall. I was also going through a difficult time with our younger son, Brandon, which made things even harder. He was not eating well and was having digestive problems that needed medical treatment.

Without going into all the details, everything was accomplished (thank goodness for my mom and dad's help). Jon finished his work in Singapore and was able to come home that September. However, when everything finally settled into place, I, unexplainably, became unsettled.

You would think I had it all together. I had a wonderful family, a new home, a new car, and a new start to life, but I was drained and exhausted. It wasn't so much the move that exhausted and emptied me; it was something far deeper than that. It was like moving back to the United States had triggered something in me; I was lonely and confused. Even though I was so blessed to have all that I had, there was a huge, unexplainable void in me that couldn't be denied. Because I didn't understand why I felt that way, I felt completely lost. I became very anxious and even had several anxiety attacks. I couldn't eat, and my weight dropped drastically. I could no longer take care of my boys, and I was desperate for help. My mom even had to stay with me for a while, until I was well enough to handle my responsibilities.

This unexplainable void was probably the darkest time in my life. Before, my life seemed fine because I had always been comfortable and "secure," but this feeling I now had could not be soothed with anything—not even with family, friends, or activities. Even though I felt hopeless, there was still a fire in me that was not willing to settle for the direction in which I was heading. Determined to find my way again, I went to doctors, read books, looked for friendships, exercised, and even looked to my family to "rescue" me. These things helped for a little while, but it wasn't until God led me to His divine path of truth that I finally began to find my way.

At the time, I didn't realize God was using this void to draw me to Himself (John 6:44). Between my persistence and God's tugging, I was finally led to His Word. I had no idea how lost I was in life until He found me. Hitting rock bottom made me realize I couldn't and shouldn't do life on my own.

During this time of searching, my good friend Nanda invited me to a Bible study. The irony of this is that my mom had been asking me for several years to join a Bible study, but I never did. I was somewhat drawn but never willing to go. So God used my anxiety and Nanda, who I highly respected and didn't want to disappoint, to get me where I needed to be. Sometimes we all need a little encouragement (and sometimes even a little push) to get us out of our lost state.

God was so good to me at that time because even though I was unsure and reluctant to follow His lead at first, He didn't give up on me. I am so glad and relieved that I finally did respond to His lead. I can't imagine what my life would be like right now if I had not responded to Nanda's invitation. I can honestly tell you that this book would not have been written, and the opportunity for you to be impacted through it would have been lost if I had chosen not to learn about the Bible. Again, I am so glad I made the decision, even though I was unsure at the time, to commit to hearing what God had to say to me.

Just like I was, many people today are apprehensive to hear and know what the Bible says and to attend a church so they can learn how to find their way according to God's Word. We either feel inadequate in our Bible knowledge or unsure about what we will learn and what kind of people we will meet. It is scary to jump into something unfamiliar.

When I first joined Bible Study Fellowship, I didn't know much of anything about the Bible. I didn't know what it really meant to be a Christian, let alone the difference between a Jew and a Gentile. I didn't understand why the nation of Israel was such a big deal. I never knew Jesus was transfigured in front of Peter, James, and John—they actually saw Jesus in His full glory. I never knew we were made in God's image. I never knew that because of Adam and Eve's sin, we were all predestined to be sinners. And I didn't understand the truth about God's holiness.

I learned something new every week at Bible study. It was amazing to me. Not only was I learning new truths, but also I was meeting new people. I met women who were set apart for God. I learned what it looks like to live for Christ and be set apart for God's glory. There was something different about some of these women, and God used them along with His Word to teach and nourish me. He slowly began to fill that void deep inside of me.

Even though I had a great experience learning about God through Bible study, I know many people who have been hurt by the church and who have witnessed Christians living in ways that are contrary to God's Word. Instead of experiencing God, they experienced condemnation, as if God's truths are something to be force-fed. They didn't experience the kind of love John writes about in 1 John 3:18: "Dear children, let us not love with words or tongue but with actions and in truth."

I want to encourage you, in spite of what you may have experienced that seemed contrary to what the Bible says; don't let what others do define who you think God is. Don't allow what others have done hold you back from what God has in store for you. Ask God to help you find a place where you can not only study His Word but also where it will be done in love—not just with words but with actions and in truth.

Until we begin to realize how lost we are without God, it will be difficult to find our way. And until we see our desperate need for Christ, we will continue wandering in the void of our lost state.

So, how will you begin to look to God for direction? What worldly map do you need to hand over to God?

God's Compass

Back in the days before maps, GPS, and the Internet, many people used a compass to find their way. According to Wikipedia, a compass is a navigational instrument for determining direction relative to the earth's magnetic poles. It consists of a magnetized pointer (usually marked on the north end) that is free to align itself with the earth's magnetic field. Basically, a compass would guide the traveler in the right direction as long as the pointer was aligned to the north end of the compass.[1] I love what Wikipedia says about the pointer: it is free to align itself with the earth's magnetic field. It made me think of John 8:32 in a deeper way: the truth will set (lead) you free if you align yourself to Jesus.

Before being led to God's Word, I aligned my compass everywhere but to the "north end" (Jesus). I aligned west, east, and south by using people, myself, and the world as my references of direction. I didn't really consider God in any of my life decisions. I thought of Him when I went to church or when someone mentioned Him, but I never looked to Him to guide my daily life. Instead, I had a good compass of morals guiding me, and as long as I did the right thing, I was confident in my own guidance. That is why I was so confused when we moved back from Singapore. I had done what I thought was right, but I felt completely lost. As I said before, that was when I knew something was wrong.

It is at our low points that we finally realize we weren't meant to do life on our own. We tend to think following Jesus is for desperate and loony people who can't handle the stresses in their lives. But I praise God for my trials and anxieties that made me realize how much I need Him.

Knowing God through His Word is like having your own personal roadmap. Even though it is universal and for everyone, it directs us individually in the particular ways God speaks to us through it. When we ask Him for direction, He will guide us, but it may not be on the path we expect. God guides us with an eternal perspective. His compass is not like the temporary compass of the world. We tend to spend our lives searching for happiness and anxiously wait for our next ground-breaking achievement. But I have learned that God is more concerned about our holiness and our relationship with Him than He is about earthly achievements and worldly happiness. Now don't get me wrong; God will answer our prayers and help us with what we need, but His top priority is our relationship with Him.

You will have to do some undeniable soul-searching to know which compass is guiding you. This means examining your motives before making a decision. Are your motives centered on you and other things or on God? How are you and others growing closer to Christ through your actions? Are you letting God guide your steps, or do you look to anything but God to be your compass? These are just a few questions that will help you determine whether you are on God's path or your own path.

Seeing God on the Journey

Many times we are running fast but getting nowhere. We run and run, but in the end, we have nothing to show for it. It's kind of like lighting a firework. We light it, watch it blow up, and then we forget about it and move on to the next firework.

Do we ever think about what motivates us to do what we do? A good example of this is playing sports. Jon and I don't involve Justin and Brandon in sports because we want them to win or be the starting player. We put them in activities as a tool to teach and train them in the way they should go. We like it when Justin has to compete for his baseball catching position—it teaches him that he is not always going to get his way all the time and that he has to work for what he wants. We teach them how to deal with disappointments when they lose or strike out. Sports and other activities have been great parenting tools to mold their identities, and it has become a way for us to spend time together as a family.

We also take very seriously our responsibility to teach our boys the Bible, which has eternal value. We want them not only to know God's Word, but also to live it and to one day pass it down to their children. This is an activity that will bear lasting and eternal fruit. Not only will their lives be blessed and changed forever, but also others will be impacted. I especially like it when we can incorporate what they are learning at Bible study with their everyday activities. Justin has used several Bible verses in his prayers to help him with baseball and school. Brandon has sung several songs glorifying God in front of others. He has also prayed for his extended family and friends to know Jesus like he does.

Reaping lasting benefits reminds me of a quote I once heard that has stuck with me and has actually become one of my life goals: "I am not afraid of failure but of succeeding at something that doesn't matter." This really made me think about how I spend my time and energy. I don't want to busy myself with things that have no lasting value. I make a commitment each day to make the most of my time. I don't have to be saving the world every moment of my day. Instead, I just need to embrace what the Lord has given me and seek His guidance so that I can follow Him as I walk through each day. Now don't get me wrong; God has called me to do things I never would have seen myself doing before—like speaking at a woman's conference or even writing this book. So whatever I do, whether big or small, I try to listen for God and be sensitive to what He leads me to do.

How do we know if what we are doing is worth our time and energy? How do we know if what we do today will last through tomorrow or next year or even for eternity? Isaiah 40:6–8 helps us to answer these questions:

All men are like grass, and all their glory is like the flowers of the field. The grass withers and the flowers fall, because the breath of the LORD blows on them. Surely the people are grass. The grass withers and the flowers fall, but the word of our God stands forever.

Just like grass, we will wither away, but God's Word will stand forever. If you know, believe, and live God's Word, you will leave behind eternal fruit. Everything else will wither away. That is what it means not to fear failure but to fear the kind of success that will eventually fade away.

Can you name someone who won an Olympic race 50 years ago or someone who won an Academy Award 25 years ago? Probably not (I know I can't). Those who did win may have been known back then, but their successes eventually faded as time moved on. Their names were slowly forgotten, and just like grass, their success withered away.

On the other hand, everything done for God's kingdom will last forever. God never forgets those who whole-heartedly live for Him and according to His Word. In fact, God will test with fire everything we do and reward us accordingly (1 Corinthians 3:14). Even when others may not appreciate your efforts as you strive to live by His Word, God sees, and He will remember. "So whatever you do, work at it with all your heart, as working for the Lord, not for men, since you know that you will receive an inheritance from the Lord as a reward" (Colossians 3:23–24).

So many times, our focus and perspective on the world gets in the way of seeing God's will for our lives. Instead of solely focusing on this journey called life, we should focus more on God while we are on the journey. If God is our focus, then the journey is just the instrument we need to experience Him. Our family, our country, our friends, and our activities were only meant to be blessings along the sidelines as we journey to see more of God.

I often tell myself that I shouldn't walk to get somewhere; I walk to see my Lord. This has really helped me to focus on Him in everything I do—from washing dishes to leading a Bible study to caring for others who don't seem to appreciate my efforts. If He is my focus, then my eyes are open to see His blessings in everything I do. I used to look at cleaning my home as a chore, but now, with God as my focus, I see my home as His gift to me. He has privileged me to care for my home and those who live in it. I can feel His pleasure when I clean my home. I also feel His pleasure when I honor my husband and lavish my children with love. God has gifted me with so much, and I need to cherish the privileges He has given me—especially when He gives me the opportunity to be a light in this dark world. I am forever grateful that He entrusted me with His gifts and His kingdom work.

Even though there is a journey for all of us to run, we have to know without a doubt that we are in the race that allows us to focus on God. We can't begin conditioning ourselves or running the way God intends for us to if we are not on board with Him through Jesus Christ. Jesus is the way and the truth and the life. No one comes to the Father except through Him (John 14:6). Notice that this verse doesn't say that Jesus is *a way*. It says that Jesus is *the way* and that no one gets to God except through Jesus. The only way to see God as we journey through life is through Jesus.

As we journey on this side of eternity, Jesus is our path, God is our focus, the Holy Spirit is our guide, and heaven is the finish line. When we finally cross the finish line in heaven, there will be no more running. We will bask in God's glory—it will be a beach vacation for eternity. "The city does not need the sun or the moon to shine on it, for the glory of God gives it light, and the Lamb is its lamp" (Revelation 21:23).

Before I studied the Bible, I thought a person's soul would just float around in a place called heaven. I didn't understand the reality of hell and that just as heaven is an actual place, hell is also an actual place. I also learned that not all people go to heaven. In fact, the gate leading to hell is a lot broader than the gate leading to heaven: "Wide is the gate and broad is the road that leads to destruction, and many enter through it. But small is the gate and narrow the road that leads to life, and only a few find it" (Matthew 7:13–14). It has been so eye-opening to study about heaven and hell in the Bible. Paul refers to heaven as the third heaven—a place that is beyond the earth's atmosphere and beyond outer space. Revelation 21 talks about heaven in very specific detail. I highly recommend you spend some quiet time reading over those beautiful verses.

Heaven is more of a reality than earth is, and it is beyond our limited imaginations. First Corinthians 2:9 says, "No eye has seen, no ear has heard, no mind has conceived what God has prepared for those who love him." Many people limit themselves to their own wisdom and miss out on placing their faith in Jesus Christ because they haven't sought out His truth wholeheartedly.

Even though we will not understand God's ways fully, we have to purposefully seek and place our faith in what God has made known and available to us through His creation and through His Word. God wants us to fully rely on and trust in Him. He knows our minds are weak and we will not understand everything (Proverbs 3:5-6). In fact, we can't handle the reality of the spiritual realm. It is way beyond what we would even want to understand. Anytime the Lord or angels appeared to people in the Bible, they would fall down as if dead (Exodus 3:6, Judges 6:22-23, Isaiah 6:5, Luke 1:12 and 2:9, Matthew 28:4). We can't handle knowing and seeing everything God does. That is why it is so important to study what God has made known to us and trust Him in those things that are hard to understand.

When God is our focus, we will begin to see and understand what God knows we can handle at the time. And as we embrace what He gives to us, each step we take will bring us closer to Him. It is literally a step-by-step journey as we grow in our relationship with God. So don't worry about what tomorrow will bring. Focus on where God has you today, and take in what He gives you each moment, because He knows that is all you can handle.

How do you see God as you journey through life? What things are causing you to hang out on the sidelines instead of running hard after God?

Running Hard after God

Abraham is one of the greatest biblical examples of what it looks like to run hard after God. He was chosen and set apart by God to be the father of God's people. Abraham was and continues to be known as a man of faith, and because of his obedience to God, he was the first man God called and used to form the nation of Israel. It is through the nation of Israel that a Messiah was going to come to save God's people (both Jews and Gentiles). But to begin this nation, God had to start with someone, and He started with Abraham.

> The LORD had said to Abram, "Leave your country, your people and your father's household and go to the land I will show you. I will make you into a great nation and I will bless you; I will make your name great, and you will be a blessing. I will bless those who bless you, and whoever curses you I will curse; and all peoples on earth will be blessed through you."
>
> —Genesis 12:1–3

Why would God ask Abraham to leave his country, his people, and his father's household? God had a plan. Not only did God want to divinely and abundantly bless Abraham, but also He was going to bless the whole human race through Abraham. God promised Abraham that his offspring would be like the number of stars in the sky (Genesis 15:5). But before God could bless Abraham (and the world), Abraham had to leave behind the "your" things in his life for the things of God.

God had to be Abraham's number one focus. Abraham had to be removed from those things that would distract him and pull his attention away from God. So Abraham was commanded to leave his country, his people, and his father's household, and he had to go to the land God showed him. The things in Abraham's life had to be replaced with the things of God.

If Abraham had chosen to stay in his country, with his people and in his father's household, he never would have had Isaac, who never would have had Jacob, who never would have had twelve sons, who never would have established the twelve tribes of Israel, who never would have established the nation of Israel. It was through the nation of Israel that people like Moses, King David, Mary, and Joseph came. It was also through the nation of Israel that a Savior was to be born (see Matthew 1:1–16, the genealogy of Christ).

Now imagine what would have happened if Abraham did not do what God asked him to do. I am sure God would have found another willing person to work through, but do you see the importance of putting God first in your life? He wants to impact the world through you, just like He did with Abraham.

The first thing on God's list for Abraham to leave was his country. As I reflected on why God would ask Abraham to leave his country, I thought about my own experiences of traveling and moving to other countries. Scotland was the first country I ever visited. When we first arrived, I was extremely timid and terrified to drive the Scottish way—on the left side of the road. The only way I knew to drive was on the right side of the road, with the steering wheel on the left side of the car. I quickly realized that not all countries do it the "American way."

So there I was, driving on the opposite side of the road with the steering wheel on the "passenger side." To make matters worse, I had to fearfully face roundabouts that were located at almost every intersection I crossed. My first attempt at mastering this circus ring was not a positive experience. I quickly realized that getting off a roundabout is not as easy as getting on. As I drove around and around, trying to maneuver toward the outside lane so I could get to the street of my destination, the drivers were not getting any nicer. I finally put on my big-girl pants and worked my way in. After several more attempts on the roundabouts in town, I adapted to the Scottish way of driving. It didn't come easily at first, though. I had to learn and adjust. When I got home to the US, I never again complained about the Houston interstates.

We also had several opportunities to visit other countries while we lived in Singapore. Bali, Indonesia, was one of the countries that impacted me the most. As we drove from the airport to our five-star resort, we saw families living on the side of the road in what looked like cardboard boxes. Their homes were made of pieces of tin and cardboard. As we drove by what seemed to be the reality for many Balinese, I couldn't help but wonder what life was like for them. Here we were driving to get to our resort so we could relax and enjoy the beautiful beaches of Bali, and there were people living in conditions that I never had been exposed to. After taking several tours and visiting a handful of villages, my little perspective and "world vision" had been broadened and stretched.

After traveling and living overseas, I realized the glaring contrast between my life and the social, economic, and traditional ways of those living in other countries. Sometimes we can get so settled in our "small-world" ways and our country's traditions and political matters that we lose sight of God's eternal picture. We can even get more caught up in the American Dream than in the dream God has for us. Second Corinthians 4:18 says, "So we fix our eyes not on what is seen, but on what is unseen. For what is seen is temporary, but what is unseen is eternal."

Imagine if we all prayed this every day: "Lord, give me Your eyes today and align my heart to the eternal things that are unseen. Decrease my sight from the temporal things so I can see You and be led to Your eternal ways." Our lives would be changed forever. And so would the lives of those around us. When our eyes are focused only on temporal things, it is hard to see from God's global-eternal perspective. We can easily get fixated on our country's traditions rather than on God's traditions and on our own activities rather than on God's activities. We tend to blend in with our secular surroundings rather than set ourselves apart for God's glory. I am not saying we should not value our country or that God is calling everyone out of their own countries. I am saying, however, that when we are fixated and focused on just our own worldly surroundings, it will limit God from working in our lives and doing what He wants to accomplish through us. David Platt wrote about this in his book *Radical*[2]:

> The key is realizing—and believing—that this world is not your home. If you and I ever hope to free our

lives from worldly desires, worldly thinking, worldly pleasures, worldly dreams, worldly ideals, worldly values, worldly ambitions, and worldly acclaim, then we must focus our lives on another world. Though you and I live in the United States of America now, we must fix our attention on "a better country—a heavenly one." Though you and I find ourselves surrounded by the lure of temporary pleasure, we must fasten our affections on the one who promises eternal treasure that will never spoil or fade. If your life or my life is going to count on earth, we must start by concentrating on heaven. For then, and only then, will you and I be free to take radical risk, knowing that what awaits us is radical reward.

Abraham did just that. He radically obeyed and followed God. And I am one of many who have been blessed by him. Galatians 3:29 says, "If you belong to Christ, then you are Abraham's seed, and heirs according to the promise." Just as God radically blessed Abraham and the world through him, God wants to radically bless you and others through your obedience. Whether or not God is calling you out of your country, if you are distracted by the power, wealth, entertainment, and politics of your own country, you may be hindering God's call on your life if you do not seek Him.

The second thing on God's list for Abraham to leave was his people. Even though Abraham was leaving his family and friends, Genesis 12:5 says, "He took his wife Sarai, his nephew Lot, all the possessions they had accumulated and the people they had acquired in Haran." Abraham wasn't totally alone. He was accompanied by his wife, nephew, and the people they had acquired, probably servants to Abraham. Apparently, the people Abraham did leave behind were those who he really didn't need to accomplish God's calling. Or it could have been that God now wanted to bless others, apart from those family members, through Abraham. Either way, God was calling him to leave his people.

Just like Abraham, we all need people in our lives who can accompany us on this divine journey. But there are also people whom we need to leave behind. A runner wouldn't want someone running with him who would trip him or lure him onto the wrong path. In the same way, we don't want to be distracted or hindered by others as we walk with the Lord.

Rather than having God as the sole commander of our lives, many of us tend to put our "peeps" on the loveseat with God. As humans, we are very relational people. That is the way God made us. He wants us to share His love with each other and to be connected. The problem comes when we try to replace God with people or when others hinder God's calling on our lives. (It's easy to hang out with others when we are having such a good time.) Our families and friends weren't meant to hinder our walk or satisfy us in ways that only God can.

When people lure us to a comfort that limits God in our lives, they could be getting in the way. We may spend more of our time and energy with them than we do living for and looking to God. We have to be careful that we are not relying more on people to fulfill us than we are on God.

God may also want to bless other people through you, which may require you to leave the people you love and value so you can make His love known to others. Yet, you can be sure that God will not only comfort and provide for you during this transition, but also He will abundantly bless your obedience in following Him.

The third thing on God's list for Abraham to leave was his father's household. This is a big one for many folks. Leaving our homes and families is hard. It was the hardest thing for me to do when we lived overseas. The day before

22

we moved to Singapore, we stayed overnight at my parents' house. The next morning, the van picked us up to take us to the airport. Jon put the luggage in the van, and we said "good-bye" to my parents. My younger son, Brandon, was not even a year old yet, and Justin was only three. My parents had moved to Houston less than a year before, and here we were moving their only grandkids to the other side of the world. As we drove away that early morning in November, all I could see was a silhouette of my parents waving good-bye. We didn't even make it to the stop sign before the tears poured uncontrollably from my eyes. Jon held me tightly and gave me all the assurance he could, but I just couldn't help myself. I was going to miss my family so much.

Just like other people, our families can limit our dependence on God. They can become our root of comfort, or they can hurt us. Either way, they can be a distraction from God's best. I once read that the good is often the enemy of the best. So many times we settle for the temporal good rather than sacrifice and seek a little more for God's eternal best. The comforts of friends and family are "good" at doing that. Some of us have such wonderful families that we have been clouded with goodness. It is really hard to see God's grace through the clouds of good things. Just like our groups of friends who make us feel good about ourselves, our families can become our comfort and even our god.

My family was my god until I met and fell in love with the one and true God, Jesus Christ. I felt His love through them—it was the closest thing I had of Him until I fully embraced where that love was coming from. First John 4:19 says, "We love because he first loved us."

There are also those who have been burdened by their families. Not only have they been hurt and wounded by them, but also God's grace has been obscured by affliction and pain. We see so many misguided and unloved children in the world. They have no concept of God's love because they have been hurt and confused by people living in their own homes. It's almost like going up to bat in a game of baseball with two strikes already counted against you. It's hard to embrace the game of life when you're at such a disadvantage. But there is always hope. As long as we have the light of Christ, we can be lifted out of our darkness. That is why God calls His children who have embraced His love to reach out to the lost. Lost people need to see and feel His love through us. Sometimes it's those very children who were afflicted at home that end up sharing the love of Christ with their lost parents. Only God's truth can do such a beautiful thing.

Just like Abraham, before any of us can be led by God, we must first be willing to be led. God never forces us to do anything. Rather, He created us with the ability to make our own choices. Until we choose to let go of those good comforts and commit to God's best, we will miss out on seeing Him more frequently and being blessed more abundantly. (Others will miss out on being blessed by you too.)

Abraham, his offspring, and the whole world have been blessed by his willingness to walk in faith on the journey God laid before him. Walking with God will be the most amazing adventure you will ever experience. This is because walking with Him becomes less about you and more about God.

Are you willing to let go of the good things so you can experience God's best? How will you begin to seek His face as you walk today?

CHAPTER 2

The Truth about Your Life

Since the Beginning

EVERY EXPECTANT MOTHER prepares for her newborn's arrival. Once she knows the baby's due date, the "to-do list" begins:

- Call family and friends.
- Pick out a name.
- Register at Babies R Us®.
- Choose the necessary items for registry.
- Paint baby's room.
- Start eating healthier.
- Buy and read books to prepare for pregnancy and birth.

This to-do list continues throughout the whole pregnancy, but inside the mother's quiet womb is a baby who has no idea of all the plans that are being made for his or her arrival. All the baby has to do is grow and arrive on time, and even once the baby is born, he or she totally relies on his or her parents for care and nurture. When the baby is hungry or not feeling well, he or she cries for feeding and comfort from Mom. What a beautiful thing.

Our life with God is the same way. He is our divine parent, who made plans for us before we were even born. In fact, Jeremiah 29:11 says, "For I know the plans I have for you, declares the Lord ... plans to give you hope and a future." God knew us before He even formed us in our mother's wombs (Jeremiah 1:5). It is God's pleasure and His right to create us for His purposes. We were not created to live for ourselves. We were also not meant to do things on our own, without God's guidance and wisdom. Just like a child looks to a parent, we are to look to God for our identity, comfort, feeding, and direction.

Many of us wonder why we are here. It is the million-dollar question. But this question can't be fully embraced unless we understand the phenomenon of creation. In the beginning, before humans walked the earth, God had a plan—and it all began with His Spirit hovering over the waters and four little words: "Let there be light." With that phrase, God began to display His glory (all of His attributes) not only to the world He would create but also to the whole spiritual realm (the angels and demons). Genesis 1 is where it all started:

> In the beginning God created the heavens and the earth. Now the earth was formless and empty, darkness was over the surface of the deep, and the Spirit of God was hovering over the waters.
> —Genesis 1:1–2

At first glance, these verses may not seem like much. But if we were to study them in great detail, we would see so much truth behind these two sentences. I love the way Tony Evans, in *The Battle is the Lord's*,[3] explains it (please note that we will discuss some of these truths more deeply in later chapters):

> Notice the familiar statement in Genesis 1:2 that "the earth was formless and void, and darkness was over the surface of the deep." To put it another way, earth was a garbage dump, a wasteland. Everything was sort of floating together in a formless mass. It was a swamp. Later God had to separate the water from the dry land.
>
> How did the earth become that way? It likely happened when Satan was thrown out of heaven and down to the earth. Whatever Satan takes over becomes a garbage dump, including our lives ...
>
> The earth became a place of judgment because it became the holding cell for Satan and his angels until such time as their sentence is to be carried out ...
>
> Satan and his demons, the fallen angels, were limited to earth and its atmosphere as their primary realm of operation. They are still spirit beings, so they have access to the spiritual world. But their primary sphere of operation is earth.
>
> So God decided to fix the wasteland called earth to demonstrate something very important to Satan and his demons and to the angels in heaven. Therefore, "The Spirit of God was moving over the surface of the waters" (Genesis 1:2).
>
> God began to bring order out of the chaos. He created light to counter the darkness. He separated the waters

from the dry land and began to dress the earth and fill it and the sea with all kinds of creatures.

Now let me show you what happened when God began to create. In Job 38:4–7, God asks Job where he was when God created the earth. God says when the angels saw His creative power, they "sang together" (v.7).

Here were the angels of heaven, perhaps thousands of years after the fall of Satan had taken place. They saw light come to the dark earth, and they rejoiced. God was going to do something. What was He going to do?

God was going to make a creature of lesser stature than the angels to demonstrate to all the universe that even though this creature did not have angelic ability, angelic power, or angelic experience, if this lesser creature would trust and obey God, he would go farther than an angel in heaven who refused to trust God.

Isn't that amazing! Since the beginning, God wanted to do something through us, a weaker creature that would surpass the power of any fallen angel. Not only would God be glorified through those who trusted and obeyed Him, but also the whole angelic realm would see His glory through humankind.

God wants to use you to reveal His character to the whole creation (in heaven and on earth). Do you realize how valuable you are? Anytime you give yourself over to God in what you think, say, and do, God gets the glory—not only with those around you, but also in the whole angelic realm. And that is why we are here: to bring God glory. Ephesians 1:11–12 says, "In him we were also chosen, having been predestined according to the plan of him who works out everything in conformity with the purpose of his will, in

28

order that we, who were the first to hope in Christ, might be for the praise of his glory."

In the Bible, we also learn that even the angels long to look upon us so that they can learn more about God and the redemption of humankind (1 Peter 1:12). It is amazing to me how angels learn about God through us even though they are in heaven with Him. That is because the angelic realm had never experienced God's grace until Adam and Eve brought sin into the world.

It was at the fall of mankind that God introduced His undeserved grace for the first time. God said to Satan, "And I will put enmity between you and the woman, and between your offspring and hers; he will crush your head, and you will strike his heel" (Genesis 3:15). God made it known in this verse that even though humankind sinned, He was going to provide a way for them to be made right with Him again by crushing Satan (death) with the offspring (Jesus) of the woman (Mary). We see this promise fulfilled through Jesus Christ—at His birth and at the cross. We see at the cross that even though Satan struck Jesus' heel, Jesus crushed Satan's head by overcoming every temptation without sinning (Hebrews 4:15). Therefore, Jesus became the perfect sacrifice for our sin. Jesus shared in our humanity so that by His death He might destroy him who holds the power of death—that is, the devil—and free those who all their lives were held in slavery by their fear of death (Hebrews 2:14-15).

Just as death came through a man (Adam), the resurrection of the dead comes also through a man (Jesus). For as in Adam all die, so in Christ all will be made alive (1 Corinthians 15:21-22). This is the ultimate demonstration of God's grace. "Where sin increased, grace increased all the more, so that, just as sin reigned in death, so also grace might reign through righteousness to bring eternal life through Jesus Christ our Lord" (Romans 5:20–21).

The reason grace is such a big deal is because without it, humankind could not be given the opportunity to be forgiven. When we sinned, we sinned against God. And nothing we can do could ever make up for our disobedience, no matter how hard we try. So God graciously provided the way that not only would redeem us from sin's power but also satisfy His judgment against it. Sin couldn't just be swept under the rug; it had to be paid for, just like crime has to be paid for.

So when sinners place their faith in Jesus, they are redeemed through His death, given life through His resurrection, and transformed by His Spirit. And this is how sinners like us are able to bring God glory. We turn our lives over to Him so He can save us and sanctify us. It is only our obedience to and trust in God that allows us to be a display of His splendor.

What does this mean for you? It means that you are extremely valuable. As you begin to discover who you are in Jesus Christ, you will begin to live the life God intended for you. And when you live for Christ, it brings God glory. Even though you were born a sinner, you can still have a relationship with God. He has provided a way for you to have life in Him. All you have to do is look to Christ to forgive you so you can start living the life God intended for you.

How will you begin to look to God's redemptive plan? Do you see the eternal value your life has through Jesus Christ?

An Irreplaceable Life

My two boys are such a crucial part of my life, and I cannot imagine what it would be like without them. They each have their own unique ways about them. Because each is his own person, they are irreplaceable. Nobody could replace them; nor would I want anyone to try. I love Justin's laid-back personality and how calm he can be in whatever life brings him. And I am so blessed by Brandon's passion for life and compassion for people. They are both set apart and impact different people in different ways.

Besides my two boys, there are other people in my life who could not be replaced. The love my husband has for me is irreplaceable. I don't think there is another man who would spoil me as much as Jon does. He loves me like no other and is such nourishment for me.

My mother is another person who is irreplaceable. She is my best friend and knows every detail about me. She has always believed in me, even when I doubted myself. She is a safe place for me. I can call her any time, and she will never turn me away.

There are so many people who have made an impact on my life who could never be replaced. I love them all—even those who made my life difficult. God used those people to help me focus more on Him.

In the same way, there are people that only *you* can uniquely impact. Every relationship we have is like a display of art, each one crafted and presented in a different way. You may draw out things in someone that nobody else could. And someone else may draw out things in you that nobody else could. That's why it is so important to be careful about what we are drawing out of others and what others are drawing out of us. We want our lives and the lives of others to be painted with God's beauty and His truth.

A crucial part of our divine journey is to know without a doubt that our lives are valuable to God. Without having a passion for our lives, it will be difficult for us to move forward in the way God intended us to.

I had never really thought about my own life being wondrous and valuable until I had a discussion with my ten-year-old son one afternoon by the neighborhood pool. Our hot Texas afternoon together was supposed to involve swimming and relaxing by the pool, but instead, it turned into a deep discussion on the miracle of life. Most of us parents never really want to discuss with our children how they were born. We (especially us mothers) would rather keep their minds free from "the talk" as long as we can. But my son chose this particular afternoon to pick my brain about how babies are formed.

His inquisitive mind started off with wanting to know if Jon and I got to choose when to have him. Once he realized that he was planned and that he just didn't appear on his own, the conversation became deeper—sperm, eggs, and embryos. After hearing about how an embryo is formed, my son wanted to know if he would have been born if Jon and I had decided to have him a year before. I had to explain to him that a year before, he would have not been born because it would have been a different sperm and a different egg.

The conversation went on for about thirty minutes, and the more I talked, the more I realized that each individual life really is a miracle. I guess I had never looked at life the way my son was making me look at it that afternoon.

After talking with my son, I discovered that each individual (not just any person, but each individual) being born is not an accidental thing that just happens. If you think about all the necessary ingredients needed to make a life, it seems simple. You need a sperm and an egg. But if you think about all the different combinations and possibilities, creating a life can get very complicated. With more than six billion people in the world today, the chances of your father meeting your mother—just one of the necessary combinations needed to make you—are pretty slim. And once they were together, the chances of that sperm meeting with that egg at that particular time to conceive you is another complicated combination.

After doing some basic research, I found out that the entire period in which an egg and sperm can unite is less than twenty-four hours, and that only one percent of the two-hundred- to five-hundred-million sperm even make it to the uterus. And even then only a few hundred or a few thousand make it to the upper part of the fallopian tubes, where fertilization can occur. Fertilization is a miracle in itself.

Life really is a miracle. The chances of you being born are indescribable. Only a Divine Creator could make this possible. Just as we look at the universe in amazement, we can look at the conception and birth of a child and see that it is remarkable. God wanted us to know without a doubt that He is our Divine Maker: "For since the creation of the world God's invisible qualities—his eternal power and divine nature—have been clearly seen, being understood from what has been made, so that men are without excuse" (Romans 1:20).

You can look at a lamp and know without a doubt that it was made by someone—it didn't just evolve on its own for no purpose at all. A lamp was fashioned by man to give light. Its unique parts include a plug, a cord, a stand, a socket for the light bulb, a switch to turn it on and off, and a lampshade. When you see a lamp, you know its exact purpose and the function of each part and how they all work together.

In the same way, yet more complex, each one of us has been created for a specific reason and by a Divine Creator; we didn't just derive from something or evolve by some random particles coming together. Just look at our eyes as an example. They are specifically designed for sight. Without each part (pupil, cornea, iris, retina, optic nerve, and so forth), we would not be able to see.

Our bodies are another great example. We can observe the parts (arms, legs, head, feet, hands, chest, knees, elbows, fingers, and toes) and know that each one was created for a reason and they all work together for a common purpose. And then you can look inside each of those parts and see how they function and relate to one another. We can even go as far as looking at all of our different systems: circulatory, respiratory, muscular, nervous, and digestive.

In short, all of God's creation was intellectually designed and fashioned with value and for a purpose. You wouldn't tell your eye it was not needed or your arm that it just evolved that way. And you certainly wouldn't tell your heart it is replaceable. No! If your parts are important to you, imagine how important you are to God.

A Purposed Life

Most parents have a natural inclination to let their kids know they are loved and valued. Parents naturally want their children to succeed and be the best they can be. For example, let's say a parent has twins. The twins may look the same, but they will each have their own personalities. A parent would collectively love them, but individually, he or she would nourish them based on each one's strengths and weaknesses.

God works the same way. He knows we are collectively created for a purpose, but each one of us has a unique personality. God loves us all the same, but He nourishes and uses us in different ways (based on how we were individually made).

God wants you to know that you have purpose in the specific ways He wonderfully and fearfully designed you.

That is why He made you like nobody else and why no one can tell you what you were specifically created for (they're not your creator). You are designed by God, a custom-made creation. You are precious and unique, not because of what you do or who you are married to or what car you drive or even how someone treats you, but because you are a creation of God—made in His image. That is what makes you special.

In fact, it is not pleasing to God when we question Him as our Creator:

> Woe to him who quarrels with his Maker, to him who is but a potsherd among the potsherds on the ground. Does the clay say to the potter, "What are you making?" Does your work say, "He has no hands?" Woe to him who says to his father, "What have you begotten?" or to his mother, "What have you brought to birth?" This is what the LORD says—the Holy One of Israel, and its Maker: Concerning things to come, do you question me about my children, or give me orders about the work of my hands? It is I who made the earth and created mankind upon it. My own hands stretched out the heavens; I marshaled their starry hosts."
>
> —Isaiah 45:9–12

God doesn't mind when we question Him with a genuine heart or when we really want to gain understanding about our lives. In fact, it pleases the Lord when you seek Him with all your heart. What He doesn't like, however, is when we question Him with defiance and judgment that defame or undervalue God's character or how He made us. God is our Potter, and He can design us as He pleases and sees fit.

Imagine having to knit together every person—each one in his or her own unique way. That is exactly what God did with each of us. Psalms states, "For you created my inmost being; you knit me together in my mother's womb. I praise you because I am fearfully and wonderfully made" (Psalm 139:13–14). I can't imagine trying to put together a person. I have a hard enough time just picking out what I am going to wear in the morning. Imagine all of the unique details that must go into creating a life—not only the physical attributes (skin, hair, and eye color; height; and body type), but also the inner person (abilities, gifts, demeanor, and personality).

Think about the complexity of just knitting a simple blanket. It takes patience and diligences to get one loop hooked to another loop and at the same time orchestrate the design and color(s) of your masterpiece. When we look at a scarf or a blanket, we often fail to notice the tiny details that make it up—the time and effort and creativity involved. Yet, according to the Bible, that is exactly what God did when He was creating us; He wove us together stitch by stitch, detail by detail. Knitting together a person is incomprehensible compared to knitting a blanket, but God is our Divine Maker, and He has knitted each one of us. If you were to die today, no one could replace you. God has designed and purposed your life just for you and nobody else.

I never really saw the value of my life until I started to know God personally. From my own perspective and from the way the world treated me at times, I saw myself as simple and awkward. I didn't have an elaborate personality that fit world's "cliquish" standards, and I wasn't beautiful enough to make up for my lack of personality. And even though I didn't want to be someone I was not, I also knew I could never meet the expectations of other people.

So instead of settling into what people wanted me to be, I choose to isolate myself to some degree. However, I later found out that isolating is just as bad as conforming to the world. Instead of letting people define me, I was letting my own thoughts define me, which were based on what I thought others thought of me—it came around full circle.

It wasn't until God started showing me how to be beautiful in Jesus Christ that I began to understand why He made me the way He did. Instead of relying on others and my own thoughts, I made Christ my focus and identity. I also began to learn that He loves me in specific ways that are particular to me. I now can see why He made me shy and introverted. I have learned that shy people tend to be good listeners and are keenly aware of those around them. Introverts tend to be deep thinkers and really take the time to make decisions instead of acting on first impulse. When I value how God made me and use my different traits for His glory, I am satisfied. It is then that I see the true purpose of my life—it is for Him, not for people or myself.

You may struggle with the way you were made. Maybe you are looking at yourself from the way others see you or from the way the world defines beauty. If that is your focus, you will always struggle. You will either battle with dissatisfaction or you will become mechanical to whatever or whoever is dictating your life.

If you struggle with who you are or with discontentment, ask God to help you understand why you feel this way. You can ask yourself a few questions: Who are you living your life for—yourself, others, or Jesus? What situations or people cause you to feel insecure or dissatisfied? Maybe it is those things you need to focus less on by putting your focus on God.

Meeting Yourself

Think of a friend or a loved one who brings out the best in you. For me, it was my husband, Jon. Being with him was the most satisfying thing I had ever experienced (this was before I knew the Lord personally). I felt so safe with Jon, and he loved me for who I was. I felt accepted and appreciated by him. We enjoyed each other's company so much—we still do to this day. Jon was independent. I didn't have to take care of him like a mother (which I had done in previous relationships). He owned his own car and was putting himself through college (he wasn't lazy or complacent). He exercised and took care of himself. He was my equal; he valued what I valued. We brought out the best in each other. Meeting Jon was one of the best things that ever happened to me. I liked who I was when I was with him.

Think about that person who brings out your best. Or maybe you could speculate on what it was like for that person to meet you. What attributes did you bring out in each other?

What if you had the chance to meet yourself? Deeper still, what if you could meet a better version of yourself, the person God created you to be? Think about if you had the chance to meet her today—right now. What if you could spend the whole week getting to know her: talking with her, laughing with her, and even crying with her. Do you think she would be someone you are striving to become? Even though your sinful nature would not allow you to be completely like her, would your life at least be pointing in the direction of her life? Are you becoming the person God had in mind when He knitted you?

Even though we will never be perfect until we are with the Lord in heaven, our best often comes out as we spend time with God and grow in our relationship with Him. It is not until we come to know God that we truly come to know ourselves. One of my daily prayers is that God would align my heart to His will and that I would be sensitive to His leading so that I can come to know who I need to be.

Our lives were meant to be perfectly aligned with God. We were meant to be one with God. We were created not only to depend on God but also to enjoy every moment with Him. Just because we failed doesn't mean God failed. Through Jesus Christ, we were able and are still able to rely on God because He always has the best intentions for us.

How are you striving to become the person God created you to be? Who are you surrounding yourself with—those who draw you closer to God or those who draw you away from God?

A Life Not Aligned with God

Before I knew how to walk with God and be aligned with Him, I was malnourished and desperately dependent on others. For most of my life, I exchanged God's truth for lies (mainly because I didn't know what the truth was). Instead of putting God on the throne of my life, I exalted myself and exchanged His guidance for my own wisdom, which caused me to believe a lot of lies. Looking back, I can see God's hand over my life, even though I was not seeking Him. But there were definitely some decisions I made that were not God-honoring.

I had several boyfriends as a teenager who I latched onto for security and self-worth. I know so many women who look to men to define who they are. They are so desperate to be loved that they replace their image in Christ for an image that attracts the opposite sex. I was one of those women. I am so grateful that I have been forgiven and now can reconcile my image in Jesus Christ. My beauty comes from Christ now. He allows and even demands me to be me, and that is the most freeing place to be.

Until I met Christ, I battled hard with who I was. As I mentioned earlier, I didn't like who I was around others. I wanted to be one of those girls people looked up to—like those who were elected for class president or prom queen (people who seemed to have a purpose). I didn't feel I had the qualifications to be one of those girls.

When I was a child, my dad had a job with an oil service company that required us to move every two to three years. Any time he was promoted or when they needed him elsewhere, we would be asked to relocate. We moved so often that as a teenager I went to four different schools. I was so grateful for my family during those moves. My home was a safe place for me, but the torment came when I had to attend a new school. Because I was shy and always seemed to be the new girl at school, I was often overlooked and ignored. I didn't have the personality I thought I needed to fit in.

Over time, my thoughts took over my identity. I would get so paranoid about what others thought of me that I would torment myself. While others were busy chatting with their friends at lunch, I was off sitting by myself—alone in my thoughts. It seemed like everyone else was having a good time and living normal lives, but I was the new girl who nobody really knew. I remember feeling so uncomfortable while waiting for the bus at the end of the day. Although everyone else was busy talking or playing with friends, I was counting down the minutes for the bus to arrive. I often sat alone thinking: *They are looking at you. They know you are sitting all by yourself. You are stupid. Nobody is going to like someone who is all by herself.* I felt so unworthy of anyone's attention, and because nobody paid me much attention, I decided for others that they didn't like me. Instead of being excited to meet people, I would put up a wall, thinking people wouldn't like me in return.

As I look back on this, it is sadly amazing how powerful my thoughts were and how dependent I was on what other people thought of me. It upsets me to think about how I stayed withdrawn in my thoughts for so long. I had isolated myself and didn't give people a chance to know me.

In the torment of this daily battle, I longed to be in my loving and secure home at the end of the day. My parents and my brother had always lovingly accepted me for who I was. I didn't have to be someone else. Because the days at school exhausted me emotionally, I wearily dropped my walls when I got home, and I was free to be myself (which is probably why my family never knew the internal torment I was going through).

One year in high school, I begged my mom to pick me up after school each day so I wouldn't have to wait for the bus. Every afternoon when I saw her car at the end of the road, I felt such relief. I could feel my mask peel off as I walked to the car. I didn't like feeling this way—in fact, I hated it. I valued and longed to be part of a group with my peers. My peers were very important to me, so much so that I had made them my god. People became my sole focus and attention. They became who I looked to for my identity.

You may have gone through an experience similar to mine or something totally different. You may have been (or still are) basing who you are around your circumstances and the world instead of around God. There is good news, though. We can get back on track with God, and God can restore the years we were off the track (Joel 2:25). It's never too late to embrace the life God intended for us. When you stop looking at everything else and start looking to God, you will begin to discover the abundant life God has for you.

Are you ready?

CHAPTER 3

The Truth about Truth

BEFORE SOMEONE CAN become a doctor or a police officer, the person has to be taught and trained for that line of work. There is usually extensive studying involved, along with a dedicated commitment to become qualified as a physician or police officer. A person can't just wake up one day and say, "I am a doctor," or "I am a police officer." He or she would have to go through a qualification process before even partaking in either of those careers.

Knowing truth works in a similar way. We can't go about our days thinking we know what truth is if we haven't really committed to know it. Yes, some of us have morals and good judgment, but is that all we are relying on? I wouldn't want to have surgery done by a doctor who only *thinks* he has a good idea of what it takes to get me better. I would want to know without a doubt that he is qualified and skilled to perform that particular surgery.

Without a willingness to study and know what truth is, we can't begin to see ourselves truthfully. We may see ourselves in light of our basic morality and good judgment, but what if we are limiting ourselves? Or worse yet, what if we are harming ourselves?

In the Bible, Jesus not only says it is His truth that sets you free, but also He says He is the way, the truth, and the life and that no one comes to the Father except through Him (John 14:6). However, many people believe Jesus was just a prophet and a humanitarian; they don't consider Him to be the one and only Messiah. They don't realize this belief is impossible. If Jesus claimed to be the Messiah but was only a prophet and humanitarian, He would have to be considered a liar. There is no way Jesus, who claimed to be the Son of God (Matthew 26:63–64), could be only a prophet. He is either who He says He is or He is a liar. And if He is a liar, then He couldn't have been a true prophet. Those people who believe Jesus is only a prophet have not studied the Scriptures and do not fully understand what they believe.

This is why it is so important to evaluate what we really believe to be true. God is not out to confuse us, nor does He expect us to come up with our own belief system. Why would God, our Maker, who doesn't need us but desires to have a relationship with us, create contradicting truths for us to live by? He wouldn't need to nor would He desire to. God has made Himself and His absolute standard of truth known, and He makes this information known in the Bible.

The Source of all Truth

Truth finds its origin in God and its preservation in the written Word of God, the Bible. The Bible is God's Holy Word. It is God's autobiography. It is His love letter to us. The Bible is how we learn about God and who He is. It is absolute, which means that it is not limited by exceptions; it is perfect in quality. The Bible is also universally for everyone who desires to know it.

The Bible was penned by men but authored by God Himself. Second Timothy 3:16 says that *every* part of Scripture is God-breathed, which means it was given by His inspiration. The Holy Spirit inspired each author as he wrote the words.

The Bible is a collection of sixty-six books that were written by forty different authors over a span of sixteen-hundred years. Moses wrote the first five books of the Bible, Genesis, Exodus, Leviticus, Numbers, and Deuteronomy. John wrote the last book of the Bible, Revelation. Moses and John did not know each other. In fact, Moses had been dead thousands of years before John was even born. So it is not likely that Moses and John (along with all the other authors) got together to have a Bible-writing meeting. In fact, many of the authors never even laid eyes on each other. It is only by the grace of God that the Bible has been put together the way that it has.

The Bible is the whole truth. It can't be picked apart or skimmed—it must be taken as a whole. Just like yarn is woven together to create a blanket, the Bible is woven together from the Old Testament to the New Testament with Jesus as the common thread throughout. From Genesis to Revelation, God's divine truth is made known for anyone who wants to know it.

Many people call the Bible the Living Word. That is because it radically transforms us as we receive it wholeheartedly. In fact, there are no other books that were written more than three-thousand years ago that still speak to us today like the Bible. Think about it: why would so many people want to read something that is challenging, convicting, hard to understand at times, and written so long ago? Because it is the only book that offers eternal hope! Only the work of God's Spirit through His Word can move people in such a way. If it didn't move people, the Bible would have died out a long time ago.

When we naturally receive God's Word like a baby receives milk from his mother's breast, we can't help but be fed. When we take in His Word in the manner it was meant to be received, it will change the way we see, hear, think, feel, walk, and speak. The Bible is unique, set apart, one of a kind, undeniable, and it demands a response.

Relative and Indifferent to Truth

Why do I go on about this? It is vital that you know what truth is. The whole purpose of my wanting to write this book was to help others understand the value of God's Word. It is His truth that will set you free. It is His truth that will transform you into the beautiful person God desires for you to be. Without it, you will be left to your own thinking, to your own desires, and to the influences around you.

Many people have a relative belief system, which means they believe whatever they want to believe. Wikipedia defines it like this: "Relativism is the concept of points of view having no absolute truth or validity, and has only relative, subjective values according to differences in perception and consideration." Basically, relative truth is loosely based on morals, perceptions, and considerations, and it is subjective to one's own opinion. Relativism is like a free-for-all—anything goes. You can believe some of God's truths, based on what appeals to you, but you can also consider your own thoughts and feelings and even add a touch of manmade religion—kind of like an a la carte or buffet of your own truth. You can choose whatever you like based on your tastes and appetite.

Just so you know, this is not what God, the Creator of truth, had in mind for His children. Like I said earlier, He is not a God of confusion. He is a God of order and makes it very clear who He is and who we need to be. As Scripture says, "God is not a man, that he should lie, nor a son of man, that he should change his mind. Does he speak and then not act? Does he promise and not fulfill?" (Numbers 23:19).

If you want to know what it looks like to be relative and indifferent to truth, the Bible has plenty of examples for you. Pilate, the Roman governor who sentenced Jesus to be crucified, is a great example of what it means to be indifferent to truth.

Before His crucifixion, Jesus was questioned and tried by Pilate. Even though Pilate had been given several signs to show him that Jesus was innocent, He still dismissed the truth that was before him. Not only did Pilate receive a warning from his wife (she had been given a dream about Jesus—see Matthew 27:19), but also his own conscience lay heavily on him. He knew Jesus was innocent. In fact, he wanted to release Jesus and let Him go, but he allowed the pressure of the crowd to sway him away from truth.

In John 18:37–38, we see that Pilate questioned Jesus one last time:

> "You are a king, then!" said Pilate.
> Jesus answered, "You are right in saying I am a king. In fact, for this reason I was born, and for this I came into the world, to testify to the truth. Everyone on the side of truth listens to me."
> "What is truth?" Pilate asked.

Pilate sarcastically questioned Jesus: "What is truth?" He did not believe there was such a thing as absolute truth. He believed truth was relative and inaccessible. He had Truth standing right in front of him, but by his own decision, he chose to ignore and ultimately compromise Jesus. Pilate was casual toward, detached from, numb to, disinterested with, uncurious of, unconcerned with, and withdrawn from truth.

Many of us are like Pilate. In fact, our society is plagued with "Pilates." Instead of looking to Jesus, we look to find truth that is relative to our own situations, personalities, culture, families, friends, and feelings. It's like going on a shopping spree for truth—a little of this, a little of that. The next thing we know, we have fitted and created for ourselves our own truth.

There are also those of us who run away from any sort of truth. We don't want to face truth at all (especially the truth about ourselves), so we pretend it is not there; we ignore it. In reality, what we have done is created our own truth that "we don't need truth." It is a vicious and wasted cycle. Truth demands a response. Every person makes a choice to know truth or not to know truth.

Do you choose to know what God's truth is? I challenge you to really think about this. It has eternal consequences, and I'd hate to think you didn't even bother to research this for yourself. Satan's greatest lie is that you don't need God's truth. He will distract you from finding life in Christ. He distracts you from knowing and studying God's Word. He will distract you from living out truth so you don't have an impact on others. Satan will relentlessly work for this and camouflage himself in any way he can; he will even masquerade as an angel of light (2 Corinthians 11:14). He does this by coming across as "religious" or "good," and he will even use religion and our own "goodness" to distract us with the lies of his half-truths. (We will talk more about those later.)

I recently watched a television program where a young woman was deceived into thinking she didn't need to face the reality of her credit card debt. (She had spent too much on clothing and other things.) She just wanted to pray to

God and trust His provision instead of facing the reality that she had been living beyond her means. Yes, God wants us to depend on Him, but we are not to test Him with our disobedience and our overindulgence. And we are not to look to God just to see what He can do for us. It is more about having a relationship with Him. If all someone wanted from you was what you could do for him or her, you would feel used and underappreciated. That one-sided relationship would never grow. Having a relationship with God works the same way. We can't knock on heaven's door and expect God to provide for us when our hearts really don't want to know Him personally. God knows those who are genuinely His, and He knows them by name (2 Timothy 2:19; John 10:3).

Another example of relative truth is how so many people think they are going to heaven, but in reality, most of them have no idea what it really takes to get to heaven. I was one of those people. For years, I thought I was going to heaven. Yes, I believed Jesus died on the cross, but I also wrongly believed that because I was a good person, I was going to heaven. In reality, this is not what gets me or you to heaven. The way to heaven is in acknowledging that we are sinners in need of a Savior. Being a good person is a lie; we are all sinners, and compared to God, we are not good. Tony Evans, in *The Kingdom Agenda*,[4] says it like this:

> The only difference between "good" sinners and "bad" sinners is the state of their decay and decomposition. The bum on skid row and the non-Christian uptown are equally dead. One is dressed better, but both are dead without the life of God.

I know this may be harsh for many people to hear, but this is how we are deceived. Satan wants us to compare ourselves to each other instead of looking to God as our standard.

Another way the Enemy masquerades his lies is in making us believe we have to work our way into heaven. He will lure us into thinking our water baptism and our good works of religion are the means to our salvation. If that were true, then we are saying *what we do* could earn us a ticket to heaven. When we believe this lie, instead of placing our faith in *what Jesus did* for us, we place our faith in ourselves and in our churches. Water baptism is not the means to salvation, but rather a symbol of our commitment to Jesus Christ. Just like a wedding ring is not the means to marriage but rather a symbol of commitment to marriage. We don't commit to Christ by what we do; we commit to Him by placing our faith in what He has done.

Now don't get me wrong; faith by itself, if it is not accompanied by action, is dead (James 2:17). But we don't want to confuse the difference between what it means to be eternally saved and what it means to be sanctified (which we will talk more about later).

We can look at the criminal on the cross next to Jesus and biblically see what it means to simply place our faith in Jesus. Because this criminal admitted and repented of his sins and then placed his faith in Jesus, he was saved. Jesus told him, "Today you will be with me in paradise" (Luke 23:43). That man didn't do anything to earn his way to heaven. All he did was confess with his mouth, "Jesus, remember me when you come into your kingdom" (Luke 23:42), and believe in his heart that Jesus could save him from his sins.

These are just few examples of how the Enemy distracts us from knowing and understanding God's truth. So, what is distracting you from knowing truth? How will you begin to hear what God has to say to you?

Desiring to Know Truth

Instead of sarcastically asking, "What is truth?" like Pilate did, some of us may genuinely want to know what truth is. You may be asking, how do I know what truth is and is not? There are so many different "truths" and religions out there. There are people who put their faith in Buddha. There are those who believe in Allah. There are universalists, who believe that as long as you are genuine in your faith, you will get to heaven. You may be thinking, *Who am I to say they are wrong and Jesus is the only truth?*

God's truth is not based on our sincerity, our feelings, or even our own wisdom. Truth is based on what God, the creator of truth, says. You might think you can fly, but that doesn't mean you can. It is impossible for humans to fly unaided. God did not create us to fly. In the same way, God did not create us to make up our own truth based on our own wisdom and sincerity. God created truth and has made it possible for everyone to know Him.

Choosing Your Faith in a World of Spiritual Options[5] by Mark Mittelberg is a great book to read if you want to understand and compare the different spiritual selections the world tends to offer us. He explains it like this:

> In a world of spiritual options, people constantly tell us what to believe. In fact, many Christians are convinced that their beliefs are right simply based on what parents and pastors have taught them. But your beliefs determine how you live. Are you choosing wisely?

He explains how people form their faith and how we can explain why we believe what we believe. I highly recommend that you read this book if you have doubts about the Bible or your own beliefs.

Sometimes it may seem that other religious or non-religious organizations are on the right path. They come across as nice and seem to speak with truth and sincerity. I recently watched a news report that told how a group of atheists gave money to a Christian church that had been vandalized. As I listened to both the pastor and the atheist, I was caught off guard, wondering why an atheist group would help a Christian church. The atheist went on to explain that he doesn't need Jesus Christ or God to be nice. His statement confused me, so I asked God to help me understand how someone like that man, who doesn't believe in a God, could be kind to someone who does believe in God.

The next morning, God helped me understand this through a local pastor on television. This pastor's teaching was on how other religious or non-religious organizations may live and speak of biblical principles, but they don't give credit to the source of that truth. This pastor went on to say that all truth comes from God—even kindness.

Whether we recognize it or not, we can think we are walking in "truth" but still miss understanding that all of those things originated with God. That is why some people, like that atheist, can be kind; he took hold of God's truth of kindness. However, even though his acts of kindness temporarily helped another, they were not done to glorify God. Instead of magnifying God, he glorified either a cause or himself.

Glorifying others or a cause gives glory to the created rather than to the Creator. This is exactly what Lucifer did. He glorified himself and the cause of his pride rather than God. If we really desire to know truth, we have to not only know it and live it, but also we have to know where it comes from so we can give God the glory—not the things created by Him.

Testing Truth

Once we accept and begin to understand God's truth, we must learn to test everything against it. We need to test what we hear about God, Jesus, the Bible, our salvation, and even ourselves and others. We shouldn't just believe anything and everything we hear, read, or think.

> Do not believe every spirit, but test the spirits to see whether they are from God, because many false prophets have gone out into the world. This is how you can recognize the Spirit of God: Every spirit that acknowledges that Jesus Christ has come in the flesh is from God.
> —1 John 4:1–2

If you are unsure about what you are hearing, reading, thinking, or doing, ask yourself a few questions:

- Does this line up with Scripture?
- Is this who God says I am?
- What would Jesus do or think about this?

Just like you try on clothes before you buy them to make sure they fit, "try on" truth to make sure it fits the image of Christ. Attending church or a Bible study is one way to try on truth. Search until you find a church or a Bible study that you can relate to and that "fits," but use discernment. The Bible says there are many false and misleading prophets—even those who "preach" in the name of Jesus. Ask God to lead you to a church that speaks about and models His true character. If a church loves in truth and in action, you are in the right place. The Bible says you will know them by their fruit (Matthew 7:20). Look for not only what is being said but also for what is being demonstrated through their actions—especially in regard to the pastor.

I remember being at one church where the priest rudely handled my son while he was trying to take communion. It was not a positive experience for us. I am not saying he was a false prophet, but his actions definitely were not those of Christ. It's important to be diligent about finding a place where you will feel comfortable and loved so you can not only saturate yourself in God's Word but also fellowship with other believers.

Also, be careful about letting others be your main source of understanding God's Word. Books, Christian speakers, pastors, and Bible study teachers are all great sources of truth, but don't let them be your only source. We tend to listen more to people than we do to God while spending time alone in the Word. We enjoy hearing stories and illustrations from other people. These stories help us relate to God's Word. This can be a good thing, but make sure you are not there more for the person than you are for God.

Sometimes we can also be lazy in our time with God. We would rather have someone spoon feed us than make the effort to see what God has to say to us personally. Either way, you don't want to miss out on the fullness of what God has to say to you. He may have specific truths in His Word just for you that you may not get by listening to others.

A good way to get into His Word is through an in-depth Bible study. This will provide you with personal, one-on-one time with God. Bible study is also great because you not only get time alone in the Word, but also you get the guidance and fellowship you need to understand those sometimes difficult passages. There are also Bible study books you can do with a friend or with your spouse. If you go this route, be very prayerful for God's wisdom and understanding as you study His Word. Learn how to rely on Him and not your own wisdom or that of your spouse or friend.

False Perceptions: Half-Truths Equal a Whole Lie

Whether you are studying the Bible or not, how do you know if what you perceive is true? Many times, our perception becomes our reality. What we think becomes our truth. For years, I lived my life around my own limited wisdom. I had some Bible knowledge and a good sense of judgment and a big dose of common sense. I thought I was doing well, until the reality of God's truth showed me how lost I was. The whole truth revealed my blinded perception of "half-truths." Even today I have to fight those half-truths with the reality of God's Word.

It is often said that a half-truth is a whole lie. Our Enemy is good at half-truths; they are his specialty. In fact, half-truths were his weapon of choice that lured humankind into sin. (If you don't believe Satan is real, wait until you read more about him later.) We can learn a lot from our ancestors, Adam and Eve. We are just like them. They demonstrate to us the reality of our limited perception. Let's look at the half-truths they believed:

> And the Lord God commanded the man, "You are free to eat from any tree in the garden; but you must not eat from the tree of the knowledge of good and evil, for when you eat of it you will surely die." ... Now the serpent was more crafty than any of the wild animals the Lord God had made. He said to the woman, "Did God really say, 'You must not eat from any tree in the garden'?" The woman said to the serpent, "We may eat fruit from the trees in the garden, but God did say, 'You must not eat fruit from the tree that is in the middle of the garden, and you must not touch it, or you will die.'" "You will not surely die," the serpent said to the woman. "For God knows that when you eat of it your eyes will be opened, and you will be like God, knowing good and evil." When

the woman saw that the fruit of the tree was good for food and pleasing to the eye, and also desirable for gaining wisdom, she took some and ate it. She also gave some to her husband, who was with her, and he ate it.

—Genesis 2:16–17; 3:1–6

Here we see how Satan distorts God's truths, commands, and consequences in order to lure humankind into disobedience. He knew that if he could get us to disobey God, then we would surely die and be eternally separated from God, for God is holy.

As we learned earlier, Satan was already kicked out of heaven because of his disobedience and pride. And because misery loves company, Satan got irritated with Adam and Eve's personal relationship with God. He wanted them to be attracted to His evil ways and not to God. Satan craves God's glory, and he will do whatever he can to steal it away. Not only did Satan lure a third of the angels with him from heaven (see Revelation 12:4), but also he was now going lure all mankind to his evil ways.

You can know if you are lured toward the Enemy just by how much you are drawn to God. If your desires are less about God and more about you and the world, you may need to evaluate through prayer what is drawing you.

Another point to make from these verses is how Satan camouflages or hides himself behind God's creation, like the serpent. If Satan were to approach us just like he is, we would be terrified, almost to the point of death—he is that scary. I have read many testimonies of people who have been confronted with the rawness of evil spirits. You can even look throughout the Bible to learn about people who were demon-possessed; it is not a pretty sight. If we saw Satan and his followers for who they are, we would run as fast as we could to get away from them. That is why Satan has to be very crafty about how he approaches us. He camouflages himself with intelligence, relationships, beauty, sex, wealth, and even religion—anything that will pull our thoughts, emotions, and desires away from God.

Another lesson we learn is how Satan works in our minds. He speaks to us through our thoughts. He may use people, the world—anything in God's creation—to speak lies into our minds. Sometimes people don't even have to say anything because we deceive ourselves in what we think others perceive about us. This is dangerous because we may be tempted to speculate about things that are not true. It is best to stick with God's Word and not dwell on what others might be thinking. We have to demolish arguments and every pretension that sets itself up against the knowledge of God (2 Corinthians 10:5). The mind is where it all starts. The mind is where all arguments and speculations begin. If we can be influenced by our thoughts, our actions will not be far behind.

The very first words out of the serpent's mouth were, "Did God really say you must not eat from any tree in the garden?" Right off, Satan lured Eve to question God's authority and command. Satan was trying to work and reason lies in her mind. He didn't want Eve to *repeat* God's command. He just wanted her to *question* God's command. We see that Eve didn't respond well. She was easily influenced by the lies of half-truths. She even distorted God's original words by adding to them the phrase "and you must not touch it." If you notice, Eve also conversed with and entertained the serpent.

Jesus never entertained Satan. He always used Scripture (God's Word) to get rid of him. Jesus always recognized lies because He knew the truth. The longer we entertain the evil of half-truths, the heavier the temptation will become to give in to sin. That is why the Bible says not to give Satan a foothold. Once we do, he becomes harder to resist. Because so many people do not study the Bible, they have no idea when they are giving Satan a foothold because they don't recognize the lies (because they don't know truth).

The next lie out of the serpent's mouth was, "You will not surely die." Here we see Satan creatively question God's consequence. He wanted Eve to believe she would not die. In fact, he added to this, "For God knows that when you eat of it your eyes will be opened, and you will be like God, knowing good and evil." Again, we see Satan manipulating God's truth. He confronted Eve's identity (her image in God) and tempted her to question who she was: "you will be like God, knowing good and evil." We know from Genesis 1:27 that Eve was created in God's image, but she didn't understand that God never intended for her to know evil, which is not of God. God wanted Eve to keep her innocence and purity in Him. He was protecting her from evil. God knew evil would distort her identity and make her a person He did not intend for her to be.

This is why it is so important to obey God. You may not understand everything God commands you to do, but you can bet your life that His commands are there to protect you. When a mother tries to protect her children from harm, she knows her children will not understand. They are not mature enough to comprehend the realities of the world yet, but the mother expects her children to listen and obey so they will be protected. God works in a similar way—He expects your obedience in order for Him to protect you.

My son Justin will often jokingly call me "meanie" when I discipline him. But he doesn't understand that there is a difference between being mean and being a disciplinarian. To be mean is to hurt a person's identity; often the person doing the harm has been tricked into doing the enemy's will. However, to be a disciplinarian is to instruct and train a child according to God's Word (this should always be done in love). I often explain to Justin that if I don't teach and train him according to God's ways, I am actually doing him more harm than good.

As a mother, I want to give Justin the best possible start to life. God commanded parents to teach their children what God says and how to love Him with all their hearts (Deuteronomy 4:7; 6:5–7). Being complacent and silent can be just as harmful as being mean. By not saying anything, we allow the Enemy to have his way with our children. What is not taught or commanded can't be learned or obeyed. Just as God commanded and expected obedience from Adam and Eve in order to protect them, parents are to do the same with their own children. We are called to be the parents of our children—not their friends.

Even though God's commands were in place to protect Adam and Eve, the two disobeyed. Then, because of their disobedience, they fell into sin. And let me just note that the reason Adam is to blame for humankind's first sin is because he was given authority over Eve. He was to lead and protect Eve, but we see that he was unsuccessful in his given authority. Not only did Adam fail to instruct Eve and remind her of God's command when she brought the fruit to him, but also he went a step further and gave in to her temptation.

In the end, they both made a choice to disobey God. Adam and Eve both rationalized their decisions and compromised God's truth. Instead of desiring God, they followed their own fleshy desires that had been sparked by the enemy's temptations. They entertained the lies instead of entertaining God's truth. What started out as a half-truth (or a distorted truth) birthed into the very first sin—which brought eternal separation from God for all humankind. This was big! A temporary delight brought an eternal curse not only for humankind but also for the earth (Genesis 3:14–19).

The fall of Adam and Eve is everyone's reality. None of us is exempt from Satan's half-truths. You can turn on the television right now and be tempted with half-truths. You can look at what your friends and neighbors are doing and be tempted with half-truths. Lies are everywhere, and unless you know God's Word, you will be drawn into sin just like Adam and Eve in the Garden of Eden. Lies are what distort our image and view of things. When we are surrounded by lies and give in to them, we set ourselves up to become those lies.

What unknown lies have you been listening to? What lies have you become?

The Counselor of Truth

When sin entered the world, not only did it separate humankind from God, but also it made us hide (or run away) from God. We see this happen right after the fall in Genesis 3:8: "Then the man and his wife heard the sound of the LORD God as he was walking in the garden in the cool of the day, and they hid from the LORD God among the trees of the garden." We learn from these verses that Adam and Eve felt shame for the first time. Their sin had not only brought them shame, but also their sin had caused them to hide from God.

We are no different. As sinners, we hide from God. In fact, many of us run away from Him. Without God's intervention, we will not be drawn to Jesus. Scripture says, "No one can come to me unless the Father who sent me draws him, and I will raise him up at the last day" (John 6:44). Without God, we will struggle in our flesh to know His truth and to know Jesus.

60

Even though sin clouds our understanding and our yearning for the Lord, God graciously intervenes, in spite of our rebellion. As God draws a person into a relationship with Him through Jesus Christ, He is preparing that person to receive His Spirit. And it is the Counselor, the Holy Spirit, who gives us a desired understanding of God's truths. Jesus talked about this:

> It is for your good that I am going away. Unless I go away, the Counselor will not come to you; but if I go, I will send him to you. … But when he, the Spirit of truth, comes, he will guide you into all truth. He will not speak on his own; he will speak only what he hears, and he will tell you what is yet to come. He will bring glory to me by taking from what is mine and making it known to you.
> —John 16:7,13–14

God's Spirit helps us to relate to God and makes His Word alive and meaningful. When I was first a believer (a baby Christian), my understanding of truth was limited. I had to start off small. At first, I took in "sips" of truth like a baby. The more I grew in His Spirit, the bigger bites of truth I started taking. But before I had the Holy Spirit, I did not understand much of anything. In fact, for the first four or five months I was studying the Bible, I didn't really get it. Paul wrote about this: "The man without the Spirit does not accept the things that come from the Spirit of God, for they are foolishness to him, and he cannot understand them, because they are spiritually discerned" (1 Corinthians 2:14).

Until we surrender our hearts to Jesus, the Holy Spirit cannot dwell in us and help us to grow. Until we are born in His Spirit, God's truth will seem foolish to us, and we will stay committed to our sinful nature. I know this can be hard to believe, and you may be hesitantly wondering,

How can God's Spirit dwell in me? What makes this possible? The simple answer is: Jesus! But to understand the deeper reality of this truth, we must look at the life, death, and resurrection of Jesus Christ.

Jesus, who is God, became one of us. He left his heavenly dwelling and made His dwelling among us: "In the beginning was the Word, and the Word was with God, and the Word was God. He was with God in the beginning. ... The Word became flesh and made his dwelling among us" (John 1:1–2, 14). Jesus was not only with God in the beginning (Genesis 1:1), but also He was the incarnation of God Himself when He put on human flesh. As He dwelled among us, Jesus never spoke on His own behalf nor acted of His own will. Rather, He spoke and did only what God told Him to. Jesus also resisted every temptation and lived a sinless life. He was the perfect Lamb, sent to take away the sins of the world.

We know that because of the darkness of our hearts, Jesus was crucified for our sins. This was no surprise to Jesus. He knew He had to go to the Cross; He came to do His Father's will. But His life didn't end there. After three days, Jesus was resurrected from the dead (there were many eyewitnesses who saw Jesus after His resurrection; see John 20–21; Luke 24; Mark 16; Matthew 28). Acts 1:3 even talks about Jesus' resurrection in detail: "After his suffering, he showed himself to these men and gave many convincing proofs that he was alive. He appeared to them over a period of forty days and spoke about the kingdom of God."

After His resurrection and forty days on earth, Jesus ascended into heaven:

> After he said this, he was taken up before their very eyes, and a cloud hid him from their sight. They were looking intently up into the sky as he was going, when suddenly two men dressed in white stood beside them. "Men of

62

Galilee," they said, "why do you stand here looking into the sky? This same Jesus, who has been taken from you into heaven, will come back in the same way you have seen him go into heaven."

—Acts 1:9–11

As we read from these verses, Jesus was taken up to heaven (and the way He went up will be the way He will return at His second coming). It was after Jesus' resurrection and ascension into heaven that the Holy Spirit came upon those who had placed their faith in Jesus. The book of Acts describes this day in detail:

When the day of Pentecost came, they were all together in one place. Suddenly a sound like the blowing of a violent wind came from heaven and filled the whole house where they were sitting. They saw what seemed to be tongues of fire that separated and came to rest on each of them. All of them were filled with the Holy Spirit and began to speak in other tongues as the Spirit enabled them.

—Acts 2:1–4

On the day of Pentecost, Jesus' disciples were filled with the Holy Spirit. Shortly thereafter, Peter stood up with the rest of the disciples and preached the good news of Jesus Christ. It was through the power of the Holy Spirit in Peter's message that three thousand people believed and were added to their number that day. Because of the Holy Spirit, Peter clearly understood all the truths Jesus had taught him, and he was able to confidently proclaim them to the crowd.

When the people heard the message, they were cut to the heart, repented of their sins, and placed their faith in Jesus. Those who accepted Peter's message were baptized with the Holy Spirit too (see Acts 2:14–41). Understand this: it was not Peter's persuasive words or his enthusiasm that cut those people to the heart—it was the power of the Holy Spirit. Only God, through Jesus Christ, can penetrate a person's heart with the Holy Spirit.

As I mentioned earlier, when we place our faith in Jesus, we are redeemed through His death, given life through His resurrection, and transformed by His Spirit. The more we repent of our sins and feed on God's Word, the more His Spirit grows within us. The more He grows, the more we are able to cooperate with God. The more we cooperate with God, the more we are able to live for Him. The more we are able to live for Him, the more fruitful we become. The more fruitful we become, the more of an impact we are able to make on others. And the more of an impact we make on others, the more others are able to experience the work of the Holy Spirit. That is how the truth sets us free: we live for Him rather than for ourselves, and others are impacted by our transformation.

Do you know and believe the truth that sets you free? How will you begin to let the Holy Spirit work in you?

CHAPTER 4

Seeing Truth

Made in God's Image

MOST OF US can point out the genetic traits that have been passed down from our parents to us. Whether it is in the way we look or in the way we act, we all have some of our parents' genes in every cell of our bodies (arguably, some we like more than others). When I see a picture of myself, I see the eyes of my mom and my grandmother. When I look at my older son's eyes, I feel like I am looking at my dad. It is really neat to see ourselves in the images of our parents and grandparents.

In a similar way, we have also been made in God's image. As His children, we were made to reflect His attributes and characteristics. Just as our parents gave us life through conception, God gave us life through His breath. Scripture states, "The LORD God formed the man from the dust of the ground and breathed into his nostrils the breath of life, and the man became a living being" (Genesis 2:7). In addition,

Job 33:4 says, "The Spirit of God has made me; the breath of the Almighty gives me life."

Not only did God give us life, but also He set us apart from everything else. Out of all the things that God created, humankind was the only creation made in God's image:

> "Let us make man in our image, in our likeness, and let them rule over the fish of the sea and the birds of the air, over the livestock, over all the earth, and over all the creatures that move along the ground." So God created man in his own image, in the image of God he created him; male and female he created them.
>
> —Genesis 1:26–27

We were made in the likeness of God, having the same characteristics as God Himself. Just like our Lord, we were created worthy of honor and respect. God not only blessed us, but also He told us to fill the earth and rule over it. He crowned us with glory and honor. David described this quite well:

> When I consider your heavens, the work of your fingers, the moon and the stars, which you have set in place, what is man that you are mindful of him, the son of man that you care for him? You made him a little lower than the heavenly beings and crowned him with glory and honor. You made him ruler over the works of your hands; you put everything under his feet: all flocks and herds, and the beasts of the field, the birds of the air, and the fish of the sea, all that swim the paths of the seas. O LORD, our Lord, how majestic is your name in all the earth
>
> —Psalm 8:3–9

We were created in God's image to reflect, represent, and relate with God. We were made to be beautiful in His image and to be passionate about Him. We didn't just accidentally or unintentionally evolve into existence so that we could live for ourselves. We have been divinely and intentionally created to be set apart for a unique purpose—to have a personal relationship with God and put Him first, above all other things.

Some of us struggle to wrap our minds around this idea that we have been created in God's image—to reflect, represent, and relate with Him. But until we come to know God personally and see ourselves in His image, it will be hard to understand the kind of relationship God wants with us.

Images and Mirrors

As I thought about being made in God's image, mirrors were the first things that came to mind. Good or bad, mirrors are the very instruments we need to see that which we can't see on our own. Without a mirror, it is not only difficult to see what we look like, but also it is nearly impossible to see what we need to soften or tame to make us more beautiful (like frizzy hair or an oily face).

Mirrors are used for many purposes and even have a history of importance. Mirrors were originally made from highly polished bronze and silver in the third century B.C. The first glass mirrors were not invented until the first century by the Romans. And for most women in the twelfth century, owning a mirror was regarded as highly respectable—they did not leave home without one.

Today, we enjoy mirrors just as much, if not more. Each morning, we partner with our mirrors as we make ourselves presentable for the day ahead. We also use mirrors as we drive, looking to see what is behind us and alongside of us. We use mirrors to decorate our homes and offices. Dentists use mirrors to see behind our teeth. There are even mirrors for our own amusement that change and distort the shapes of our bodies.

Everywhere we go, there is likely a mirror nearby. Think about every bathroom you walk in. What is the first thing you see? A mirror. In my house alone, we have ten mirrors (almost one for every room). It would be interesting to know how many times we look in a mirror each day.

While writing this book, I noticed that I was more conscious of mirrors. It seemed that every time I walked past one, I was drawn to look at myself. Whether I fixed my hair or straightened my clothes, I was always trying to make sure my appearance was appropriate. Why is that? Why is it that some of us are so attracted to our image?

Pride was the first answer that came to mind. And whenever I think of pride, I think of the biblical character Lucifer. Lucifer was the greatest angel God created, yet because of his pride, his beauty turned to ashes. Many scholars believe Ezekiel 28 describes Lucifer in great detail. Even though the king of Tyre is the one mentioned in this particular passage, we can easily see that Lucifer was the spiritual power behind him.

> You were the model of perfection, full of wisdom and perfect in beauty. You were in Eden, the garden of God; every precious stone adorned you: ruby, topaz, and emerald, chrysolite, onyx, and jasper, sapphire, turquoise and beryl. Your settings and mountings were made of gold; on the day you were created they were prepared. You were anointed as a guardian cherub, for so I ordained you. You were on the holy mount of God; you walked among the fiery stones. You were blameless in your ways from the day you were created till wickedness was found in you.
> —Ezekiel 28:12–15

We see from these verses that before Lucifer's rebellion, he was a divine beauty with a capital "B". He had every reason to desire a mirror, for he was God's most beautiful and anointed creation. He was not only beautiful, but also he had an important position in God's kingdom. God had given him occupation over His garden, and he was anointed as a guardian cherub. He stood on the holy mount of God.

But we learn from Ezekiel 28:17 that Lucifer's heart became proud on account of his beauty. He corrupted his wisdom because of his splendor and, in turn, his own vanity. Basically, Lucifer looked in the mirror too long. He was so mesmerized with his own beauty that he captivated himself and turned away from God. He tried to steal God's glory because of his own beauty and position. He forgot that he was created; he was not the Creator.

God's glory could not be shared, nor should it. Lucifer didn't realize that without God's glory shining brightly around him, he would not have been able to see his own beauty. God's reflected glory brings everything into light. Because of Lucifer's rebellion against God, he was cast out of heaven and his beauty became ashes. In the end, he became the greatest Enemy to God's kingdom—he became Satan:

Through your widespread trade you were filled with violence, and you sinned. So I drove you in disgrace from the mount of God, and I expelled you, O guardian cherub, from among the fiery stones. Your heart became proud on account of your beauty, and you corrupted your wisdom because of your splendor. So I threw you to the earth; I made a spectacle of you before kings. By your many sins and dishonest trade you have desecrated your sanctuaries. So I made a fire come out from you, and it consumed you, and I reduced you to ashes on the ground in the sight of all who were watching. All the nations who knew you are appalled at you; you have come to a horrible end and will be no more.

—Ezekiel 28:16–19

Even though mirrors can be very useful and insightful, they can also be dangerous, as we saw in Lucifer/Satan's case. Sometimes mirrors can lure us to look at ourselves too long—in good and bad ways. You may look at yourself with pride and vanity, but some of us may look at ourselves and focus on every imperfection. Both situations are bad because we are dwelling on ourselves. Any time we focus on ourselves too long, it distracts us from looking to God.

Looking in a mirror and desiring to look presentable and beautiful is not wrong. Mirrors are very useful tools that help us to feel good about ourselves. God wants us to take care of ourselves. The problem arises when we believe beauty is more important than God. When our beauty (or lack there of) becomes our focal point, we are on dangerous ground. We are being set up with the temptation to put ourselves before God. God makes it clear that we are to have no other gods or idols before Him (Exodus 20:3–4).

You don't have to be beautiful to be prideful. Pride involves focusing on yourself, to satisfy or dwell on you. Unlike human beings, God doesn't dwell on our outward perfection or beauty; He looks at our faith in Him. "Man looks at the outward appearance, but the LORD looks at the heart" (1 Samuel 16:7b). How might you be focusing more on yourself than on having a heart for God?

Life Without Mirrors

As I thought about what life was like *with* mirrors, I then wondered what life would be like *without* mirrors.

I tried to imagine what my own existence would be like if I got up every morning without a tool of any kind to reflect my image. How would I put on my makeup? How would I pluck my eyebrows? How would I style and curl my hair? It would be hard to do anything without a reflected image staring back at me. As I pondered this, I decided my options were limited: I could either blindly get ready on my own, or my husband could help me. I quickly realized that my restricted options would not be ideal for me (or my husband).

As I mentioned earlier, good or bad, mirrors help us to see what we can't see on our own. They are the very instruments we rely on to make ourselves beautiful each day. But imagine if there was a mirror that did the same thing with our innermost being—a mirror that could reflect our whole personality; a mirror that could help us to be beautiful on the inside; a mirror that could tame, shape, polish, and beautify our whole inner being. This mirror would not only help us to see those things that make us beautiful but also those things that hinder our true beauty from shining forth (sometimes our personalities need to be tamed just like our frizzy hair).

We often forget that there is such a mirror. And some people don't even realize this mirror exists. We tend to pass it up every day, not even realizing we are missing out on the very reflection we need to transform our inner selves into radiant beauty queens. Instead, most of us rely on others, the world, and even our own feelings to be our mirrors. We put so much focus and energy on our outer beauty that our inner beauty gets overlooked.

God wants you to discover your true beauty in Jesus Christ. He is your divine mirror. He wants to make you up each day with His love and truth.

God's Word helps reflect Christ's beauty in you. James 1:23 describes God's Word as a mirror. You can learn about God's truth in the Bible. The Bible is our divine mirror that is written and produced by God Himself. Gazing into His truth allows us to see what God sees.

The Mirror of Truth

When a couple gets married, they make vows to each other. Their vows are not just idle words, but promises the two people intend to keep. In fact, most couples invite family and friends to their wedding not only to celebrate with them but also to witness their commitment in marriage. The reason words are spoken is so that each person understands without a doubt that he or she is making a covenant (in most cases, under God) promise to the other. They are telling each other that they will be together until the end ("till death us do part"). The words they speak are supposed to bring life into their union as husband and wife.

Unfortunately, marriages fail. The words spoken to each other in the beginning of their union become void, and the promises they made to each other become broken. Unlike people, God is a promise keeper. He never breaks a promise. We see this throughout the Bible. He is perfect and faithful to the promises He makes. Even when we sin and turn our backs on God, He still loves us unconditionally and provides a way to Him through Jesus Christ. Because God is the same yesterday, today, and tomorrow, His Word is the only constant thing in our lives and will never fail us (Hebrews 13:8). You can rely on and look to His Word at all times. His Word brings life and doesn't change. In fact, God created the entire universe with His word alone. "God said ... and it was so" (Genesis 1).

As you can see in Genesis 1, God's Word has life and brought forth life. That is why the Bible is known as the Living Word. It brings life into the depths of our darkness. It makes the temporal and chaotic nothing into an eternal and orderly something (Genesis 1:1).

Deuteronomy 32:47 says that God's words are not just idle words; they are our life. God wouldn't lie or be casual about what we need. He made it known from the beginning that we would need His Word. He knew the temptations we would face and the trials we would go through. He knew how sin would infect us and warp our identities. In fact, God told His people, "Fix these words of mine in your hearts and minds; tie them as symbols on your hands and bind them on your foreheads" (Deuteronomy 11:18). God knew we would need to carry His words everywhere we went. We would need them in our minds ("bind them on your foreheads"), we would need them in our hearts ("Fix these words of mine in your hearts"), and we would need to carry them into the lives of others ("tie them as symbols on your hands"). We need His Word, not only so we can be set free but also so we can be God's hands and feet in the world around us.

Imagine if you didn't eat or sleep for three days. Do you think you would be very productive at work or at home? Most likely not—you probably would be too hungry and tired to do much of anything. In the same way, when we deprive ourselves from feeding on God's Word, our identities become depleted. Just like our physical bodies need water, food, clothing, and sleep, our souls (mind, will, and emotions) need God's Word. When you are hungry, you eat so you don't starve. When you are tired, you sleep so you are not exhausted. In the same way, when you are fearful, anxious, dissatisfied, depressed, or worried (just to name a few), you need to feed on God's Word. If we have time to eat, get dressed, and sleep, then we have time to spend with God. God's Word is a *need,* just like food and sleep. Not only will His truths feed you, but also they will nourish and eventually transform you. Imagine what your days would be like if you spent each morning with God.

Because I didn't know God for the first thirty years of my life, I didn't have His Word as my life source. My life source came from family, friends, my thoughts and feelings, and the world around me. I remember when I first started studying the Bible. For the first four or five months, I didn't see or feel any change, but I stayed with it. Deep down I knew I needed to be in Bible study. I signed up for the next year's study, and it was during that year of studying Genesis that God's truths started having an effect on me.

When we are being saturated in God's Word, that is where the transformation takes place. You can't take one dive by going to church once a week and then get out of the pool of God's Word and expect to be changed the rest of the week. You have to soak in the Word.

As I thought about soaking in God's Word, I was reminded of those little animal-shaped sponge capsules you find on the toy aisle of Wal-Mart®. My boys loved playing with those in the bathtub. They couldn't wait to see what kind of sponge animal was inside each capsule as it soaked in their bathwater. They would wait and wait until finally a frog or a lion would stretch itself out of each capsule one poke at a time as the water dissolved its shell.

We are similar to those capsules. Each one of us has an identity just waiting to be discovered. Until we soak in the water of God's Word, we look no different than our other capsule friends. We may have different skin color, just like the animal-shaped sponge capsules do, but nothing sets us apart in the way we live our lives. Inside us is a person God wants us to discover. When we saturate in God's Word, we start absorbing His truth into our image. At first, we might not notice a change; we look the same. Over time, however, a little "poke" of something starts to come out of us. When God's Word takes root in the depths of our soul, a radical transformation starts to take place within us. It will become so evident that other people will start to take notice. My Bible study teacher, Kim, once said, "We were not created to fit in, but to stick out"—to let Jesus stick out of us. People may not understand as Jesus begins to stick out of you, but hopefully they will be drawn to know Him through you.

It takes a willingness on our part to soak in His pool of truth in order to absorb the Living Word. Soaking in God's Word doesn't mean we just sit in the "feel-good" part of His pool. We have to saturate in His whole truth—the truth about His love and provision *and* about His wrath and judgment on sin. Without knowing and saturating in the whole truth, we will only be partially transformed. It is God's desire for all of His truths to be in your innermost parts (Psalm 51:6).

I encourage you to look at your schedule today and purposefully find a way to work in some time with God. If you don't know how to begin, start by just talking to God. Ask Him how you can get to know Him better. The Bible says that you do not have because you do not ask God (James 4:2). Once you ask Him, open your eyes and your heart and expect Him to answer your prayers. You may be invited to a Bible study by a neighbor or a friend. You may be flipping through TV channels and come across a Christian program. Or you may be in the bookstore and "accidently" pass the devotionals or Bible aisle. Either way, be sensitive to how God will answer your prayers. While you wait, continue to pray. Talk to Him about what is heavy on your heart. Make God a priority in your daily schedule—He is your life.

Absorbing Truth into Your Image

We will not fully know who we were meant to be until we are in heaven. But while we are here, we can progressively begin to see our reflections with much more clarity as we start to absorb God's Word within us. First Corinthians 13:12 says, "Now we see but a poor reflection as in a mirror; then we shall see face-to-face. Now I know in part; then I shall know fully, even as I am fully known." God knows us fully. Therefore, the more we know God, the more we will begin to know ourselves.

The very first truth God absorbed into my heart came from Genesis. I learned that we were made in His image because He wanted a relationship with us. That blew my mind! I couldn't believe what I was hearing. I had such a passion for relationships (even though they were difficult for me). I had always tried to make myself beautiful through people because I wanted to connect with them. I had let them become my mirrors, but I had it all wrong. That truth taught me that beauty doesn't come from people; it comes from God. Once my relationship was right with God, then my relationships with people would be right. I didn't know this before because I never had spent time in God's Word. I didn't know what He wanted me to learn. But He knew the exact truths that would open my mind and my heart to Him. Trust me; He will speak to you too. God knows what is important to you, and He knows what truths you need to connect with Him. You just have to make yourself available to Him and open your heart to hear Him speak.

Even today, when I struggle with who I am around others, 1 Timothy 4:12 (AMP) is a truth that I focus and meditate on over my feelings of self-doubt. It says, "Let no one despise or think less of you because of your youth, but be an example (pattern) for the believers in speech, in conduct, in love, in faith, and in purity." Another verse I look to when I get down or too hard on myself is Psalm 42:5 (AMP): "Why are you cast down, O my inner self? And why should you moan over me and be disquieted within me? Hope in God and wait expectantly for Him, for I shall yet praise Him, my Help and my God."

I not only looked to verses to overcome my unstable feelings, but also I looked to other Christians who are beautiful examples of what it looks like to be a woman in Jesus Christ. My mentor and Bible study teacher, Kim, is one of these women. Not only does she teach the Word, but also she lives the Word, and I have learned so much from her. I am able to reflect a lot of God's truths in my life because Jesus pours out of her and into me. As I listened to her and other women in my Bible study pray each week, I learned how and what to pray. They modeled for me what it means to revere God and how to seek God's guidance in everything.

In the very beginning of my walk, I was taught the importance of teaching my children how to look to God. I started praying with Justin and Brandon every morning before they went to school. My husband even started noticing a change in me. He liked the way I was submitting under his authority and how I demonstrated respect to him as my husband. God's Word was changing me, and people were taking notice.

Eventually my husband joined a Bible study too, and he even took Justin and Brandon with him. As we engaged in God's Word as a family, we not only took His truths into our own individual images, but also we started to impact the lives of those around us.

You too can begin absorbing God's Word into your image. The first thing you can do is pray. Ask God to give you a heart to know Him so you will not only have a desire but also an understanding of His truths. If you struggle in your belief, ask Him to help you with any doubts you may have. The Bible tells of a man who asked Jesus to help him with his unbelief (Mark 9:24). I know so many who do not study God's Word because they either do not believe it or they think it's too hard to understand. But that is exactly what the Enemy wants you to think (remember, we are in a battle). Satan knows that when you get into the Word and start believing it, you will be changed and transformed.

Don't be discouraged, and never give up seeking to know more about our Lord. As I said earlier, the more you know Him, the more you will know who you need to be. Be purposeful and persistent to learn more about what the Bible has to say in your life and in your world.

In addition to going to church on Sundays and my weekly Bible study, I listen to Christian CDs (music and lectures) in my car. I also read books, have devotions each morning, and watch Christian programs on television. I surround myself with other believers who encourage me to live for Him and help me stay accountable to God's Word. Our resources are unlimited. None of us has any excuse not to be in His Word.

How will you begin today to absorb God's Word into your image? If you have doubts, what will you lose by studying His Word for at least a year or so? Remember, God does not need us. We need Him.

Absorbing or Force-Feeding God's Truth

Absorbing truth into your image doesn't mean you force-feed yourself with God. You don't go to church or

Bible study out of obligation or to check it off your weekly "I'm a good person" to-do list. God doesn't want our church attendance; He wants our heart attendance. God doesn't force us to love Him or to have a relationship with Him. He wants us to go to Him because our hearts desperately need and desire Him.

God also doesn't want our confessions of remorse and regret if we are not repentant in our hearts over our sin. We saw what happened to Judas, who had a heart of remorse but not repentance. Matthew 27 speaks of Judas's account:

> When Judas, who had betrayed him, saw that Jesus was condemned, he was seized with remorse and returned the thirty silver coins to the chief priests and the elders. "I have sinned," he said, "for I have betrayed innocent blood." ... Then he went away and hanged himself.
> —Matthew 27:3–5

Judas recognized his sin, but instead of repenting, he held on to his sin with remorse and regret. Sin has to be given to the only One who can forgive it. Sin that is not repented of (even though we may be remorseful or regretful) will still have its way with us. Just like Judas, without redemption through repentance, we will continue to be slaves to our sins. Even Jesus said it would have been better if Judas had not been born (Matthew 26:24).

A repentant person mourns over his or her sins and desires to turn away from evil ways. A repentant heart sees the need for God's forgiveness and is thankful for His grace and mercy. God does not despise us when we go to Him with our brokenness. In fact, it is a sacrifice to Him—an offering pleasing to Him (Psalm 51:17). He desires for us to need Him and to receive all He has for us. He wants us to pour out our burdens and brokenness at the cross, and in return, He gives us freedom through Jesus Christ.

As I said earlier, there is no need to force anything before God because He doesn't need us to define or justify His nature. He is perfect and has all He needs in Himself. We are nothing compared to God, and He is not defined by us. The good news, though, is that God chooses to "need" us because He loves us and wants to involve us in His plans.

Ask any parents if they need their child. They will say "yes" without question. It's not that they need their children to take care of them. They need their children because they have an indescribable love for them. They could not imagine life without them. The only reason we are able to love our children the way we do is because God loved us first (1 John 4:19).

Unlike some parents, God does not have a "needy" love for His children. He doesn't live vicariously through us or force us to be something we're not simply because it makes Him feel better about Himself. He is perfect in Himself and has a perfect love for His children. He finds pleasure in us when we turn to Him in thanksgiving and praise. Scripture says, "For the sake of his great name the LORD will not reject his people, because the LORD was pleased to make you his own" (1 Samuel 12:22).

Have you been trying to force-feed yourself with God? Do you live in condemnation and guilt because of your sins? God wants you to know that you don't have to force His truths into your heart. All you have to do is absorb them—just stand in front of His Word and let them come in. God does not draw you in by using guilt or obligation; that is a lie from the Enemy. God draws you with freedom and willingness to receive His love and forgiveness. You just have to look to Him so He can give all He has for you.

Absorbing or Ignoring God's Truth

Think of the last time you told your children repeatedly to do something and they didn't listen. They may have heard you and even responded to you by saying, "Yes, ma'am," but they just didn't follow through in obedience. Why is that? Do they not care? Do they not respect or fear the authority figures in their home? Are they lazy and indifferent to the requests and commands of their parents?

As God's children, we do the same things to Him. We may hear His commands, but do we really listen to Him and do what He says? Just like our children do with us, some of us not only ignore God, but also we will even argue with Him—especially if we don't like the consequences of our disobedience. God's truth and commands can't be argued with or ignored. James 1:22–25 explains it this way:

> Do not merely listen to the word, and so deceive yourselves. Do what it says. Anyone who listens to the word but does not do what it says is like a man who looks at his face in a mirror and, after looking at himself, goes away and immediately forgets what he looks like. But the man who looks intently into the perfect law that gives freedom, and continues to do this, not forgetting what he has heard, but doing it—he will be blessed in what he does.

This passage means that if we look at or read God's Word and don't really understand it or let it sink in, then it will have no impact on us. In fact, we will be deceived into thinking that we do know it just because we heard it ("do not merely listen to the word, and so deceive yourselves"). We can't just listen to (or see) His words; we have to place our faith in them and then do what He says. Ezekiel 33:31 says it like this: "My people come to you, as they usually do, and sit before you to listen to your words, but they do not put them into practice. With their mouths they express devotion, but their hearts are greedy for unjust gain."

God's truths and commands play an important role in the believer's life. They are not there just so you can study and learn from them. They are there for you to absorb and live them out. That is the difference between someone having head knowledge of God's truths and someone having a heart acceptance of His truths. When God's Word takes root, its fruit is evident in the way a person lives and loves others.

Are you listening with your head or are you absorbing God's Word in your heart? Are you doing what God's Word says? If so, how are you bearing fruit from His seeds of truth?

Finding Freedom in the Law of God's Truths

Just like a parent's discipline, God's commands are not there to "boss" His children around. God put them there to protect us and transform us into His image. They are the basic foundation of the moral law. They were given to Moses through the Ten Commandments and fulfilled and brought to perfection by Jesus Christ.

God also gave us the Ten Commandments in order that we might recognize sin as sin (see Romans 7:7–25). We would not know what is right and wrong in God's sight if we didn't have the Law. God's commands help us to know without a doubt what is sin in His eyes.

With that being said, God also knew we could not uphold the Law on our own. In and of ourselves, we are led by our own passions and desires (we don't have it in us to desire God and to be obedient to all He says). Even if we did keep most of God's commands but broke only a few of them, we still would be in disobedience. As James says, "For whoever keeps the whole law and yet stumbles at just one point is guilty of breaking all of it" (James 2:10).

God wanted us to realize that without Him, we would be slaves to the law and to ourselves. That is why His grace is such a big deal. He sets us free from what we can't do on our own. Christ is the end of the law so that there may be righteousness for everyone who believes (Romans 10:4). That is why Jesus did not come to judge us; He came to save us (see John 12:47). Jesus is the fulfillment of the Law. He perfectly obeyed the Law and fulfilled the Law's demands so that we can have freedom from the Law in Him.

I lived with condemnation for years. I tried to be perfect in front of everyone (even myself). Each time I failed, I took on another beating of self-condemnation. I always felt I was failing someone by not meeting his or her expectations. I exhausted myself by trying to live with perfection—that is because I am not perfect and never will be perfect until I am in heaven. Without knowing the grace of Christ, I looked to my own works of goodness for validation instead of looking at the reality of Christ's redemption. As God began to help me to understand what I was doing, I repented and asked Him to forgive me for trying to be perfect (to be like Him). I asked Him to help me turn away from perfection by giving Him all the expectations I put on myself. In return, He is now giving me the freedom to look to His strengths where I am weak and imperfect. It is so liberating not having to worry about what others think of me and to remove the heavy yoke of condemnation.

When Jesus died on the cross, His last words were, "It is finished." That meant everything Jesus was sent to do had been accomplished and was now available for us to receive. The only thing we have to do is reach out and receive it. Just like we have to receive and accept a gift to enjoy it, we have to receive and accept the gifts Jesus has made available to us. When we place our hope and faith in Jesus, we are free from the law of our own character and goodness. Thank you, Jesus!

Through the Holy Spirit, believers are liberated to live out God's commands in freedom—not perfectly but passionately. Even though we are forgiven, we are still to uphold the Law so we can be set free in all Christ has available for us. We don't do this in and of ourselves, but rather we allow Jesus to transform us in such a way that we become people who desire to keep the commandments.

Where we are weak, imperfect, under-qualified, and disabled; God is strong, perfect, over-qualified, and able. Our shortcomings are what should make us reliant on Him instead of on ourselves. That is why Paul gladly boasted about his weaknesses—they made him dependent on God. God's power is made perfect in our weaknesses (2 Corinthians 12:9).

Where are you depending on God? What weakness do you need to give to God?

CHAPTER 5

The Truth About Lies

Letting God Search You

THE ONE THING about a mirror that you may or may not like is that it does not lie. When you look in a mirror, it reflects back the exact image staring at it. If we don't like what we see and want to modify the reflection staring back at us, we have to make a change. We can alter our hair, change our clothes, add a dash of makeup, or even dazzle ourselves with some jewelry to become more beautiful.

Just like a mirror, God's Word does not lie. Rather, it reflects exactly what God has made known. His Word is just as revealing and honest as a reflected image in a mirror. As we gaze into His Word, we will begin to see our true reflection from God's perspective—the good and the bad. Only then can we begin to make the necessary changes to become more beautiful on the inside.

"Nothing in all creation is hidden from God's sight. Everything is uncovered and laid bare before the eyes of him to whom we must give account" (Hebrews 4:13). God sees everything about us, and one day we will give an account of ourselves before Him. Those who are in the Lamb's Book of Life will give an account of what they have done for God's kingdom and will be rewarded accordingly. Those who are not in the Lamb's Book of Life will give an account of all their sins and will be eternally separated from God (Revelation 20:12; 21:27; 22:12; 1 Corinthians 3:12–15). Until then, it is God's desire (and it should be ours) for us to see and remove those things, like pride, unforgiveness, fear, anger, and so forth, so we can begin to take on His beauty and receive His eternal rewards.

In Psalm 139, David wanted God to search him and reveal the hurtful ways in him. He said, "Search me [thoroughly], O God, and know my heart! Try me and know my thoughts! And see if there is any wicked or hurtful way in me, and lead me in the way everlasting" (Psalm 139:23–24 AMP). David wanted his integrity and devotion to God to stay true. By his allowing God to search him, those wicked hindrances would be exposed. Like David, when we allow God to search us, we are giving Him permission to reveal the ugliness we've worked very hard to hide. Once those things are exposed, God can then lead us to repentance, where those impurities can be purged.

Letting God search you is kind of like when a police officer searching a criminal. The officer takes away all those weapons that could bring injury to the offender or to others. Once the hurtful things are removed, the criminal is no longer a threat to himself or society. In the same way, when we allow God to remove those things that harm us, we and others are no longer threatened or hindered by them (our sins not only hurt us but also those around us).

Being searched by God can make us feel vulnerable, but He is not there to shame us. He wants to help and partner with us. Scripture says, "Do not be afraid; you will not suffer shame. Do not fear disgrace; you will not be humiliated. You will forget the shame of your youth" (Isaiah 54:4). Before we know who we are in Christ, we are too young and immature to understand God's ways. That is why God says, "You will forget the shame of your youth." He will teach us how to leave behind those things that brought us shame in our youthful understanding as He leads us to repentance.

As God begins to search us, He will probe and examine us so we can see what He sees. Sometimes this can be an uncomfortable process because many of us do not like to be exposed (our pride hates it). I know many adults who resist going to the doctor because they don't like to be examined and don't want to hear any potentially bad news. But knowing the bad news is better than not knowing. At least when we know what's wrong, we can start doing something about it.

Just like our sicknesses, our wicked ways will stay hidden if we aren't willing to be examined. It's kind of like testing fruit. Even though it may look pretty on the outside, the inside may be rotten. It's not until the fruit is squeezed or cut open that the decay inside is exposed. When God inspects us, He may squeeze or cut us so we can see what comes out. When you are being tested under pressure or squeezed in a situation, what comes out of you?

- Patience or impatience?
- Love or anger?
- Joy or complaining?
- Forgiveness or bitterness?
- Faith or fear?
- Mercy or revenge?
- Grace or condemnation?
- Confidence in God or worry?
- Commitment or indifference?

- Passion or passivity?
- Self-control or self-indulgence?
- Self-worth in Jesus or self-pity?
- Consideration or criticism?
- Running to God or running away from God?
- Truth or lies?

Sometimes when I am driving, I catch myself complaining about the other drivers. Instead of enjoying my ride home, my attention will be on what other drivers are doing wrong. I quickly recognize the rottenness of my complaining and ask for forgiveness. I then try to find joy in my ride home by thinking about my family or thanking God for giving me the means to drive and to own a reliable vehicle.

I also catch myself judging someone instead of praying for that person. It is so easy to judge others when we don't understand the circumstances they are in. We may judge a mother in the way she parents her child only to learn later on that her child has autism. We may consider a person snobbish only to realize later that he is shy. Being critical is so hurtful to us and to those we judge. We must quickly ask for forgiveness and then intercede by praying for them.

God reminds me that when I see individuals walking in sin and don't understand their circumstances, I am not to judge them but rather to pray for them. When we do this, it gives us a heart of compassion for those people and draws us closer to them and to God.

How do you respond to things throughout your day? What reactions do you need to place at the cross?

Letting the Mirror Expose the Ugliness

Every morning we stand in front of our bathroom mirrors, knowing that we need to make ourselves presentable for the day. At first glance, we see our pale skin, our puffy eyes, and our matted hair. But as we begin to "partner" with the mirror (by washing our faces, applying our makeup, and styling our hair), our best features come to light. In the same way, as we look in the mirror of God's Word, we partner with Him to clean up the ugliness from within. Just as it takes effort to get ready in the morning, it also takes effort to nourish our identities.

Looking at the ugliness within is something most of us don't like to do. Not only is it painful to see what is injuring us on the inside, but because most of us don't know how to cure those unseen dilemmas, we end up ignoring them. We tend to ignore the infectious jealousy and the harmful grudges we harbor against others. It's also easy to ignore our efforts to selfishly please certain people instead of focusing on pleasing God. But until we see and start to aggressively remove that cancer within, we will delay and hinder the process of our becoming who God created us to be.

I remember when God first started showing me the infection within me. I had gone to Him in prayer to help me see what was preventing me from living the life He intended for me. The next day He opened my eyes and gave me a view of my most glaring sin: putting myself and others before God. I relied so heavily on what people thought of me and I was so focused on trying to fit in that I totally left God out of the picture. This caused me to be more self-focused than God-focused. Anything we put before God is idolatry.

This self-focus led to another sin: self-pity. When I felt others ignoring or rejecting me, I would begin to pity myself. At the time, I didn't realize that self-pity is a sin. But as God opened my eyes to the reality of my being pitiful, I realized I was again dwelling more on myself than on God.

I was also consumed with fear—fear of rejection and fear of failure. I didn't want anyone to see my failures because that might give people a reason not to like me. This kind of fear was causing me to dwell on myself as I refused to trust and look to God. Doubting God is like telling Him you can't rely on Him, but we know this isn't true. We can always rely on God because He is never-failing.

Let me note that not all fear is sin. Only when you let your fears become bigger than God are you walking in dangerous territory. It is natural to fear at times—whether you have been diagnosed with cancer or you have been abused by someone. God has given us the emotion of fear. Fear makes us aware that whatever is causing us to fear is bigger than we are. This should cause us to look to God, who is infinitely bigger than what we are going through. Fear is not our enemy, but when we allow that fear to take our focus off God or when that fear causes us to be disobedient, we are giving the Enemy an opening to torment us.

Did you notice that every sin God revealed to me had caused me to focus on myself? Incidentally, the word "sin" has the letter "I" in it. Sin focuses on "I" (self). Sin caused me to look inward instead of upward. Being self-focused and people-focused was a huge burden on me, and it weighed me down.

The Ugliness of Sin

Wearing sin is like having spinach in your teeth. Even though you may not be aware of this unseen dilemma, others may notice. And even if they do take note, more than likely, nobody will point out the green speck because they don't want to embarrass you or hurt your feelings. It's not until you finally look in a mirror (which may not be until you get home) that you see the ugliness of your situation. As this undesirable reality becomes exposed, the rest of your day is ruined as you think about every person who may have been revolted when you smiled.

Nobody likes to know they are wearing "ugly." In fact, most of us are completely unaware of the sinful "spinach" we are wearing. We are blinded to our own sins until we are willing to see them. Jesus talked about this in Matthew 13:14–15:

> You will be ever hearing but never understanding; you will be ever seeing but never perceiving. For this people's heart has become calloused; they hardly hear with their ears, and they have closed their eyes. Otherwise they might see with their eyes, hear with their ears, understand with their hearts and turn, and I would heal them.

It takes Light to dispel darkness. If you are not willing to look in God's mirror, you will be oblivious to what you are wearing on the inside. If you don't let Christ deal with your sin, the ugliness of all your hurts, fears, and wrongdoings will stay on you.

My spinach example is benign compared to the reality of what sin actually does to us. Most of our heartaches and suffering are the result of sin. Sin is the wedge that has separated us from God and distracts us from loving Him the way we should. Sin injures and holds us captive. We are in exile because of sin; it not only eternally separates us from God, but also it continues to have power over us. Sin dulls our sensitivity to love others the way we should and causes us to be indifferent and lazy toward God. Sin blinds our comprehension of Jesus, and can even cause us to be repulsed by Him.

Before I was a believer and took God's Word into my heart, I was unprotected and vulnerable to sin. I was openly exposed to the enemy's arrows of lies. Without the belt of truth, the breastplate of righteousness, the shield of faith, the helmet of salvation, and the sword of the Sprit, I was nakedly available for my greatest Enemy to attack me (Ephesians 6:10–18). Without God's armor and knowing who I was in Jesus Christ, I was attacked in multiple ways. Every lie I believed was like a whip cutting me:

"You're no good" [*crack!*]; "The scars on your face make you look ugly" [*crack!*]; "You don't need to respect your husband" [*crack!*]; "You're not smart enough" [*crack!*]; "Nobody will ever like you" [*crack!*]; "You can never be forgiven for that" [*crack!*]; "You can't depend on anyone" [*crack!*]; "You sounded so stupid" [*crack!*]; "Something must be wrong with you if they are not willing to talk to you" [*crack!*]; "You don't know how to get along with others" [*crack!*]; "You didn't meet your husband's expectations—you're just not good enough" [*crack!*]; "You're bad for not doing the right thing" [*crack!*]; "You're way too under-qualified to do that" [*crack!*].

I am sure you get the point of what lies do to us (you can probably name some of your own). In fact, Isaiah did a great job explaining the effects:

Why should you be beaten anymore? Why do you persist in rebellion? Your whole head is injured, your whole heart afflicted. From the sole of your foot to the top of your head there is no soundness—only wounds and welts and open sores, not cleansed or bandaged or soothed with oil.
—Isaiah 1:5–6

As you can see, we are beaten and injured by the sins that derive from lies. Having had no protection for more than thirty years, I was pretty beat up when I finally met

Jesus Christ and started wearing His armor. As I thought about all the beatings I have taken (because of my own sin), my heart grieved to think of the beatings and crucifixion Jesus took for my sin. He did not deserve such evil treatment (whereas, I did). He was sinless and was obedient to God's commands and will. Every beating and nail given to Him was a representation of the sins He took on for us. As Scripture states, "God made him who had no sin to be sin for us, so that in him we might become the righteousness of God" (2 Corinthians 5:21). "Christ died for sins once for all, the righteous for the unrighteous, to bring you to God" (1 Peter 3:18).

Jesus was not only betrayed and denied by His own disciples, but also He was wrongfully arrested, undeservingly mocked, grossly spit on, unjustly tried by His own people, violently flogged with sharpened, bone-studded leather thongs, and *willingly* nailed to the cross, where He *willingly* died for our sins. If you study the whole horrific ordeal Jesus had to go through, it will bring you to your knees.

Mentally seeing and knowing what Jesus had to go through reminds us of the horrific and evil effects of sin. Sin is no joke, and it has deadly consequences. Without the blood of Christ covering us, there is no forgiveness and healing. And without His armor, there is no protection.

What lies are beating you down and causing you to sin? Are you wearing the blood of Christ so those sins can be forgiven and healed?

The Father of Lies: Our Greatest Enemy

Satan, who is our greatest Enemy, is behind every ugly wound we possess. I hope by this point in my book that you understand that Satan is real and his kingdom is very actively at work in our world. Not only is Satan an actual creature (Ezekiel 28), but also he is a spirit being. He has a personality and is cunningly intelligent (2 Corinthians 11:3). He exhibits emotions (Revelation 12:17; Luke 22:31) and demonstrates that he has a will (Isaiah 14:12–14; 2 Timothy 2:26).

Here are just a few verses in the Bible about Satan:

He was a murderer from the beginning, not holding to the truth, for there is no truth in him. When he lies, he speaks his native language, for he is a liar and the father of lies.

—John 8:44

The god of this age has blinded the minds of unbelievers, so that they cannot see the light of the gospel of the glory of Christ, who is the image of God.

—2 Corinthians 4:4

[Satan is] ... the ruler of the kingdom of the air, the spirit who is now at work in those who are disobedient.

—Ephesians 2:2

Your enemy the devil prowls around like a roaring lion looking for someone to devour.

—1 Peter 5:8

Satan himself masquerades as an angel of light.

—2 Corinthians 11:14

... that ancient serpent called the devil, or Satan, who leads the whole world astray.

—Revelation 12:9

For our struggle is not against flesh and blood, but against the rulers, against the authorities, against the powers of this dark world and against the spiritual forces of evil in the heavenly realms.

—Ephesians 6:12

So many times we want to lash out against other people (and even ourselves) as though they are the real enemies, but in reality, our greatest enemies are Satan and his evil kingdom.

I can now look back on my marriage and see how Satan's kingdom influenced me and my husband to inflict wounds on our relationship. It seemed the more expectations we put on each other, the more of a foothold we gave the dark world. Not only did we look at each other as the enemy at times, but also we looked at each other so much that we missed looking to God for guidance. The more we focused on each other, the more blinded we were to the real Enemy (that is how the Enemy distracts us). Satan easily hides behind people and the world (remember the serpent in the Garden of Eden).

Imagine trying to fight someone we can't see or someone who is way bigger than we are. It is impossible. Most of us tend to defend ourselves by lashing out at others and sometimes even ourselves. Fighting Satan on our own is like putting ourselves in a lions' den—there is no way we will win. We will lose every time, and we will have no way to defend ourselves.

There is good news, though. God didn't leave us without weapons. In fact, *He* is our weapon. But until we know who our Enemy is and how to use God's weapons, we will continue to fight our Enemy in our own strength (and we will *always* lose). We can't defeat Satan by resenting and lashing out at others. We can't defeat Satan by ignoring him and busying ourselves with activities and addictions. We can't defeat Satan by condemning ourselves or by worrying. We defeat our greatest Enemy by relying on and committing to the Word of God.

> The weapons we fight with are not the weapons of the world. On the contrary, they have divine power to demolish strongholds. We demolish arguments and every pretension that sets itself up against the knowledge of God, and we take captive every thought to make it obedient to Christ.
>
> —2 Corinthians 10:4–5

To fight Satan, we have to bind up the lies (take them captive) and kill them with God's truth (the sword of the Spirit). His Word is the only offensive weapon we have. All other weapons are defensive—the breastplate of righteousness, the helmet of salvation, the shield of faith, and the belt of truth. God's defensive weapons protect us, but God's offensive weapon (His Word) actually kills Satan's lies. Praising God is an even more powerful weapon—especially when we praise God in the midst of our struggles (Ephesians 6:13-18).

Until we know truth and receive it into our deepest cracks and crevices, it will be hard to defend ourselves because we won't recognize the lies (remember those half-truths we talked about). Again, that is why it is so important to know, pray, and do God's Word. Praying His truth enables us to target our attacks and shoot them down (Hebrews 4:12, James 5:16). And obeying His Word strengthens us to be more battle-ready and stronger for His kingdom (Deuteronomy 28:1).

As I began to let God heal me with His Word and started to walk in His truth, the Enemy started adjusting his battle plan toward me. I wasn't much of a direct target for the

Enemy before because my sinful nature was so caught up and distracted with the world. I didn't realize Satan had already set up his battlefield in mainstream America. Hollywood, media, popularity, money, success, and living for yourself because "you deserve it" are just a few channels the Enemy has used to trap us. It is so easy to get caught up in the mainstream because it seems like the right thing (everyone else is doing it), but we don't realize that it pulls us away from God and pushes us more toward ourselves.

Recognizing these lies is like detecting counterfeit money: it's not done by studying the counterfeits; it's done by studying and knowing what the real bills look like. After extensively looking at every detail of the authentic bills, the experts can quickly spot a counterfeit because they know what the real thing looks like. That is exactly what we have to do—we have to study and believe in the details of what God's Word says and allow it to transform our lives so we can recognize the counterfeit of lies.

How will you study and do God's Word so you can recognize the lies? What armor are you wearing to defend yourself from your Enemy?

The Battle

Many of us pray for those who are in the military—especially those who are serving overseas. We know that their lives are at stake and the sacrifices they make bring freedom to many people. Freedom has cost millions of people their lives, but in the end, many lives have been set free because of those who died.

We are in a battle—each and every one of us. Until Christ comes again, everyone is easily susceptible to Satan's army. In fact, Jesus even says that Satan is prince of this world (John 12:31). He prowls around like a lion, looking for someone to devour (1 Peter 5:8).

A prince always has an army under him. But we know that Jesus overcame Satan and his kingdom. Jesus has dominion over him because Jesus is the divine King (John 18:37). Hebrews 2:14 says, " ... that by his death he might destroy him who holds the power of death—that is, the devil—and free those who all their lives were held in slavery by their fear of death." Jesus tells us to take heart when we have trouble, for He has overcome the world (John 16:33).

Being in a battle is no joke. Lives are held captive by the penalty of sin (eternal death) until they are willing to be under the kingship of Christ. And even then, believers, His royal priesthood, are still susceptible to the influential power of sin. The battle is bloody, and every lie we believe pierces us like an arrow:

- Rejection darts at the core of our hearts.
- Peer pressure squeezes and constricts us.
- Hurtful words pierce our self-image.
- Failure cuts so deep we think it will kill us.
- Abuse from others bruises our bodies and damages our minds.
- Pride blows us up and destroys us.

All these things are traumas in our lives, but it is not the traumas that hurt us—it is the lies we believe. One thing God started teaching me was not to take on the lies others believe. If someone ignored me or was rude to me, I was not to take on their lies or the speculations that came into my mind because of what they did. Many times the failures of others can become chains we wear around our necks. Just because someone else believes lies doesn't mean we have to believe them too.

Even though you may have been a victim of abuse, you don't have to live as a victim. You can choose to live by what God's truth says rather than by the lies and sin of your abuser. You can do that by placing all those hurts, sins, and lies at the cross and relying completely on Christ for healing and protection.

We could be in the midst of some horrible storms because of what others have done to us, but we are still protected when we place ourselves under the wings of Christ. When we don't do this, those lies will hurt us. And if we don't deal with them, they will become strongholds.

Lies come from the father of lies, and every arrow Satan launches will be tipped with something contrary to God's Word. A lie is anything "that sets itself up against the knowledge of God" (2 Corinthians 10:5). When the arrows of lies hit our souls, our thoughts and feelings will feel the hit. What you do after the arrow comes your way will determine your injury (or not). You can either let the lie bounce off of you (because you are wearing the armor of God), or you can fight the lie with God's Word.

For example, if you are hit with the arrow of rejection—whether a friend rejects you or a job interviewer rejects you as a potential employee—the lie may tell you that something is wrong with you. If your mind believes and entertains the lie, it will plant a feeling of unworthiness on your soul. As your thoughts dwell on the lie (because your soul feels the rejection), it begins to manifest into sin. The sin could be self-pity or more dependence on people rather than God. It could even develop into bitterness and unforgiveness. The lie tries to sway your focus onto yourself and others rather than on to God, and that is how lies are turned into sin. Every sin starts with a lie.

On the truth side of this illustration, God may have permitted that person's rejection because He wanted to protect you from someone He knew would not be good for you. And He may have kept that company from hiring you because He had a better job waiting for you down the road, or He may have wanted to teach you to rely on Him first. We never know what God's plans are for us, but what we can know for sure is that He always has our best interests in mind and always is trying to teach us more about Himself, despite how the world treats us.

When we entertain lies, our thoughts magnify them. The more we ponder (like Eve did in the garden), the more we start to speculate and assume things that cause us to lose sight of God. If we do not fight these lies off with truth, these imaginations will turn into sin and eventually become strongholds. These strongholds are what take over our identities.

I recently watched a TV interview with a man who was on death row for raping and murdering women. He explained that what started off as watching soft porn turned into a horrific stronghold of rape and murder. I know this is an extreme example of one man's stronghold, but if lies are not taken seriously from the start, they can become the very darkness we live in and even bring us death (remember, the Enemy comes to kill, steal, and destroy).

We can't be casual with things that could eventually grow into something bigger than we are. What starts off as a casual drink every Friday night could eventually turn into a drink every night. The next thing you know, you can't stop thinking about when your next drink will be, and eventually, you become a slave to alcohol. Or what started off as casual flirting could eventually turn into a full-blown affair. If we are not fleeing from our Enemy, we may be setting ourselves up to be destroyed by him. We have to be sensitive and aware of the situations we put ourselves in.

When we allow the Enemy to have his way with us, we are giving him the opportunity to create a hold on us. These holds start off as little, enticing grips (like bait on a hook), but eventually, they can become strongholds if we are not careful. As these enticing grips loosely surround us, they begin to have an unknown, casual hold on us. As the grip slowly moves in and becomes tighter, we are clueless about the Enemy's strategic plan behind the grip. It's not until the hold has constricted us into a pit of destruction that we finally realize something is wrong. At this point, we are so imprisoned by the Enemy's lies that without the Lord's help, we are completely bound to the pit of darkness and will continue to stay there unless we turn to His Light.

To better explain the effects of these strongholds, let's use the illustration of a physical injury. If you hurt your arm, for example, the rest of your body and even your thoughts are compromised as they work around your injured arm. You become dependant on others and incapable of doing certain things on your own anymore. Similarly, strongholds not only affect our thinking and actions, but also they cause us to be negatively dependant on others and things and make us incapable of living the life God intended for us to live. As a result, we develop unhealthy thoughts, emotions, and habits and eventually become spiritually malnourished.

The Layers of Strongholds

Strongholds are like an octopus latched onto us. The many tentacles are the many layers of sin that tightly grip us. This is why we are so paralyzed and unable to bring glory to God. For years, I let what others thought about me become a stronghold in my life. What started off small manifested itself into something way bigger than I could handle. One by one, I felt the lies of rejection hit me. One arrow, two arrows, three arrows, four arrows ... I don't know at what point the stronghold became bigger than I was, but I could definitely feel the effects grow worse and worse as time went on. Not only did I believed I was unworthy, but also I didn't know how else to think. Unworthiness became my identity. Even though I had friends and family who loved me and valued me, it didn't matter. I was held captive by insecurity.

This stronghold latched onto me like a ball of sinful yarn and weaved itself into the core of my being. As God started unraveling this layering of sin in my life, He revealed one layer at a time. As I mentioned earlier, the first layer of sin God revealed to me was fear and self-pity. Those sins needed to be purged, so I repented and laid them at the cross: layer one.

The next layer of sin God revealed to me was self-condemnation. For years, I felt I had to be perfect. If I felt any inclination that someone didn't approve of me, I was devastated and would condemn myself for not meeting that person's expectations. I held on to my shame and lived a life of perfectionism. I was so worried about my own goodness that I became a slave to my character and self. Those sins needed to be purged, so I repented and laid them at the cross: layer two.

The third layer of sin God revealed to me was unforgiveness and judgment. God never intended for others to give to me what only He could give to me. Every time I tried to get these things from others, I only found disappointment and judgment. He also revealed that when others did treat me wrong, I needed to forgive them. Those sins needed to be purged, so I repented and laid those at the cross: layer three.

Stealing God's love was another thing that needed to be purged. The greatest commandment is to love God with all our hearts, souls, and minds (Matthew 22:37). My validation was being fueled when I looked at the way others loved me instead of looking to God as my first love. Don't get me wrong; it's good to be loved by others, but our first love should always be from and for God. Only then can we love ourselves and others the way He wants us to. Those sins needed to be purged, so I repented and laid them at the cross: layer four.

Over the course of four years, I repented of each layer of sin as God revealed them and God began to heal me. Things that held me captive before don't affect me nearly as intensely as they used to. Instead of being defined by how people respond to me, I now look to God for my worth and value. My fear was transformed into a radical reliance on God. My self-pity was turned into praising God. Self-condemnation and my own goodness were no longer my mirror; God became my character and my first love. Instead of judging others, I started joyfully praying for them. My unforgiveness turned into sorrow for the way others acted. Through my repentance and because of Jesus' blood, my ashes turned into beauty.

The best way to describe this radical transformation is by comparing it to birthing a child. The birthing process is painful and laborious, but all of that is forgotten when a mother sees her baby for the first time. In the same way, transformation does not happen overnight; it is a commitment and takes hard work. Even though those four years of radical transformation were a lot of work, the result has been worth every effort.

You can observe your own life for strongholds. Prayerfully make a list of your actions, thoughts, and words for one week—especially those things that cause you to feel extremely self-focused. Next to that list, write what seemed to influence your decisions, thoughts, and words. Then ask yourself: Why do I do what I do? Why do I say what I say? Why do I think what I think? What has a hold on me? Start laying what God reveals to you at the cross, and let Him begin to heal you.

Our Sinful Nature: Satan's Companion

Have you ever wondered why toddlers have such a hard time sharing their toys or why they often tell their parents "no"? They, just like all of us, have been born with a sinful nature. Not only do parents have to teach their children how to overcome their self-centered ways, but also adults have to be aware of their own selfishness. We all have a sinful nature—this is why we are so enslaved by sin. Sin doesn't just latch onto us. We have taken it on because we have allowed it in (whether we realize it or not). None of us is exempt from being a sinner. When sin entered the world through Adam, it became a reality for all people (Romans 5:12). And "if we claim to be without sin, then we deceive ourselves and the truth is not in us" (1 John 1:8).

Our sinful nature is hungrily attracted to sin. It pulls at us to satisfy and gratify our sinful cravings. Not only does it lead us to engage in what we know we shouldn't do, but also it makes us a slave to ourselves. Paul explained this very well:

> I know that nothing good lives in me, that is, in my sinful nature. For I have the desire to do what is good, but I cannot carry it out. For what I do is not the good I want to do; no, the evil I do not want to do—this I keep on doing. Now if I do what I do not want to do, it is no longer I who do it, but it is sin living in me that does it.
> —Romans 7:18–20

I never realized the power of my flesh until I committed to giving up solid food for three days by going on a liquid fast (let me just note that eating is not a sin—I am only using this as an example of how powerful the flesh is). I fasted to seek God's provision in an area of my life. In fact, it pertained to writing this book. To show my commitment to Him, I gave up my desires for His desires. After the first day, I became desperately aware of how much I needed to feed on God in order to control my flesh. Every time my stomach pulled at me and said, "I hungry," I had to seek the Lord. The more my flesh cried out for food, the closer I had to get to God so I wouldn't give in to my fleshly desires. It seemed that by the end of my fast, I was pressing into Jesus pretty hard, and His miraculous provision came through.

The reason I share this is to help you understand that God has so much He wants to give us, but the artery of our flesh tends to be plugged with sin and our selfish desires. Until we seek and press into Him by repenting and pulling away from our desires, the abundance of what God has for us will continue to be held back by sin and things of the world.

Like I did, you need to fight for your freedom! Don't let the Enemy and your sinful nature hold you back from all that God has for you. Stand up, and be radically intentional about seeking Jesus. Hear Him. Fill your mind with Him. Study Him. Saturate yourself with Him. Crave Him. Get on your knees before Him. Press into Him. Repent and ultimately live for Him. Do not be casual about this. Even if your flesh fights you, ask God to give you a desire for Him and less of a desire for the world. There is no way you can fight the Enemy or even your own flesh without the Lord's help.

How will you begin to ask for God's help? What one thing can you give to the cross so you can begin receiving His rewards?

CHAPTER 6

The Truth Shall
Set You Free

Removing the Cancer of Sin

REMOVING SIN IS similar to removing cancer. Sin, like cancer, has to be diagnosed before a sinner (patient) can be provided with the right treatment plan through Jesus Christ. My dear friend Carrie walked through the frightening and trying treatments of cancer. Not only was her body affected, but also her mind, will, and emotions were tried. Carrie describes in great detail her personal and heartrending victory over this dreaded disease:

> I was diagnosed with breast cancer in September of 2007 at the age of thirty-nine. I had no family history of this disease and no precursors to it, so the diagnosis came as a shock to me and my family. My specific diagnosis was Invasive Ductal Carcinoma, Stage 2A. My surgeon laid out my treatment plan: six rounds of chemotherapy (spaced three weeks apart), lumpectomy surgery to remove any tumor remains, and six weeks of daily radiation.

Even though my cancer diagnosis was shocking, I knew God had prepared me for this nine-month journey before it even began. I had just finished studying the book of Romans the spring before my diagnosis, where I learned a lot about God's transforming work in my life. Romans 5 spoke to me about rejoicing in sufferings, because those sufferings produce perseverance, character, and hope. Romans 8 spoke to me about how God uses all things (good and bad) for my ultimate good. And Romans 11 spoke to me about how big my God is and that from Him, through Him, and to Him are all things.

So when I heard the doctor give me the "bad" news that I had an aggressive form of breast cancer, I was not thrilled (if I had been given the option to opt out of this diagnosis, I would have done it in a heartbeat). However, since studying His Word, I knew that God is sovereign and faithful and that He was at work in my life for my good and for His glory. I also knew God can be trusted in all things, including my breast cancer. With all this weighing on my mind, I sensed that I was about to embark on a journey with God unlike anything I had ever experienced before.

In every step of my cancer treatment, I had to whole-heartedly trust God by remembering and focusing on everything He had taught me. Not only did I have to depend on God for my complete healing, but also I had to look to Him for every step in between: effective treatments, minimal side effects, protection from any infection, doctors' wisdom to treat me so that every cancer cell would ultimately be eradicated from my body. In addition, I looked to God for the well-being of my husband and two young sons, who had front-row seats to this journey.

Throughout my entire treatment, I was abundantly and overwhelmingly blessed by God ... in too many ways to mention here. Even when I experienced the ugly sides of treatment—hair loss, feeling nauseous and weak, weight loss, lack of concentration, and the inability to find words to what I wanted to communicate, God was pouring His love on me and I felt it!

Twice during treatment I experienced setbacks. The first setback was after I completed chemotherapy and was scheduling my lumpectomy surgery. Not only did I come down with the flu, but also I had to postpone my surgery because of it. I felt defeated and was upset that the calendar of events the doctor laid out was being interrupted. But God quickly reminded me that He had been faithful up to that point and He would continue to be faithful even with that delay. He was giving me the opportunity to trust Him more and to take our relationship deeper than it was. His work in me was not done yet.

The second setback came after my lumpectomy surgery. My surgeon informed me that not all of my doctors were satisfied with the pathology results. Therefore, I needed a second surgery to remove more tissue and to ensure that my margins were indeed clear. Again, I felt defeated and upset. I was so ready to move on to radiation, which was the next and final stage of treatment. I could see the finish line, and I didn't want anything to get in the way of my getting there. Even though the whole process of my cancer treatment had been an incredible experience with God, I was ready to be finished. Cancer treatment becomes all-consuming for the patient and family, and I was eager to be "normal" again and to have my life back. But God's ways are not my ways, and His plan and timing are always perfect. I got a second gentle reminder from Him that He was in control. I could trust Him for *all* the details of my treatment—even an unexpected second surgery and a timeline that was not going as the doctor said it would. God showed me that I was putting a lot of misguided hope in calendar dates and treatment timelines. Instead, I needed to put all of my hope and trust in Him, my heavenly Father.

I finally finished my final step of radiation without any complications in May of 2008—to the praise of His glorious grace. Since then, I continue to be monitored by my team of doctors several times a year, and I continue to trust God that the cancer will not return. He was gracious to me by giving me my breast cancer experience, and He proved Himself faithful to me throughout that process. For that I am so grateful.

Carrie's cancer experience not only taught her how to trust God, but also it made her realize how much she needed Him in every little, big, or unexpected step she took. Through her tribulation, Carrie was able to personally experience God in ways she never would have if she had not acquired cancer. God's Word became alive and real to her through her suffering. It was no longer just something she casually learned from Bible study.

None of us would like to experience what Carrie went through, but in the end, we would if we had to. Whether the treatment is chemo, radiation, or the operating table, those who are sick are at the mercy of the doctor's plan.

Being healed and set free from sin works the same way. Because the ugliness of lies and sin are so deep-rooted in our identities, God has to "surgically" dig them out. Therefore, we are at the mercy of God's treatment plan. He is the only One who is skilled to examine us, diagnose us, and heal us. If we are unwilling to be under His care, we will stay sick and bound. Only in Him will we find a cure and freedom. With cancer, you have a choice about whether or not to accept a doctor's treatment. If you choose not to, you put your life at risk. In a similar way, we put ourselves at risk eternally if we don't let Jesus treat our sins.

In the previous chapter, we talked about the examination process. When we allow God to search us, He will examine and then diagnose the wicked ways in us and begin to treat us accordingly. This is all part of His healing process. To be set free, we must see our sin and understand how to be healed from that sin, for it is His truth that sets us free. Without seeing, knowing, understanding, believing, and holding on to His truth, there is no true freedom.

How Sin Makes Us Sick

Just as there are many types and degrees of cancer or other illnesses, there are many types and degrees of sin. Similar to cancer, we can define sin as an evil condition that spreads destructively if not treated. Sin spreads when we choose to believe lies or act independently of God. Even though cancer is cancer and sin is sin, both can vary in intensity. For example, cancer can be categorized as stage one, a lesser degree of cancer, or it can be classified as a stage four, a more severe stage of cancer. In a similar way, even though sin is sin to our holy God, no matter the degree of it, deep-rooted strongholds (layer upon layer of sins) put a heavier yoke on us than a one-time occurrence of sin.

Let me note that God is disgusted with all sin—no matter if the sin is minor or major in our eyes (which we tend to evaluate by comparing one sin to another). All of us "have sinned and fall short of the glory of God" (Romans 3:23). Because of this divide, our sins eternally separate us from God.

The best way to demonstrate this is with a practical example. Let's say we have three cups of fluid. One cup represents God, and the other two cups represent two people who have differing amounts of sin. God's cup is pure and holy. It is filled with uncontaminated, clean, drinkable water. The other two cups are corroded by sin. For the sake of this illustration, we will use human waste to represent the sin in each cup.

Cup two represents what many would consider a good person. We will say this is Bob's cup. Bob is hard-working and loves his family very much. But there are times when he talks about other people—especially that one lazy co-worker who makes Bob's job difficult—and allows bitterness to take root in his heart. When life is going well for Bob, he tends to be more self-reliant than God-reliant. Even though he means well, he still struggles with pornography at times and lies to his wife about it when she catches him on the computer. Bob's cup is mildly contaminated.

Cup number three, however, Todd's cup, is horrific. Todd is evil. He has no regard for human life. Not only has he raped and murdered women, but also he sells drugs and steals when he needs money. There is no need to go on with his story. His cup is fully loaded with waste.

Now, let's put Bob and Todd's cups in front of you. Both are contaminated with differing amounts bodily waste. Which cup would you drink from?

This is the reality of sin to God. Sin disgusts Him no matter what the degree of it is. He can't be around it, just like you can't drink any amount of bodily waste, no matter how little. But the good news is that Jesus is our sin filter. As we give ourselves to Him, He filters out our sin and makes us clean and holy so we can be with God. He connects us back to God and heals us from our contamination of sin.

The reason I am parking on sin for a moment is because I really struggled with not only understanding my own sin, but also with understanding the intensity with which my sins were harming me. Until God showed me, I was oblivious to what was hurting me.

It is so important to know the specific sins hurting us so we can recognize what we need to give to the cross. Can you identify with any of these specific sins?

Lust	Fornication
Gossip	Stealing
Sexual impurity	Lying (giving false
Manipulation	testimony)
Adultery	Idolatry
Pride	Coveting
Murder	Dishonoring your parents
Jealousy	Strife
Anger/rage/malice	Disobeying God
Greed	Drunkenness
Homosexuality	Profanity

And let us not forget those "self" sins we don't always consider as sin: self-pity, self-reliance, self-condemnation, self-focus, self-service, self-righteousness, and so forth.

As you can see from the list above, we all sin and fall short of God's standards. We just need to let God show us those particular sins that are hurting us so we can repent and begin to be healed and set free.

What sin can you identify with in your own life? Are you willing to let God deal with that sin?

Diagnosing Sin through Conviction

My younger son hates going to the doctor. When he hears he has an appointment, the first words out of his mouth are, "Am I going to get a shot?" or "Is the nurse going to stick that thing up my nose?" He can't stand the idea of being poked and examined. Yet without that poking and examination, the doctor can't diagnose why he is hurting.

Just as doctors partner with their patients, God partners with us to help us see the things causing us harm. Even though God already knows the areas of infections, we may not. God has to point them out to us so we can seek His help. Once we see and know our injuries and illnesses, we can then understand how to work with God to get them removed.

God usually pokes our injuries and sicknesses with conviction, which will lead us to repentance without regret (see 2 Corinthians 7:9–10). If we don't respond to conviction with repentance, we will probably end up either condemning ourselves or someone else. Don't get conviction confused with condemnation. Any time we blame someone else or we feel guilty, worthless, or stupid, we are under condemnation. Those things do not align with God's Word. If we have truly responded to God's conviction and repented, then there should be no blame, guilt, or bad feeling about ourselves or others, for there is no condemnation for those who are in Jesus Christ (Romans 8:1).

It's not who we are that displeases God. It is the lies we believe and the sin we have committed that displeases Him. Condemnation finds faults in who we are, which leads to loss and death. Whereas, conviction disapproves of the sins we have committed, which leads to repentance without regret. Through repentance, the sins and the guilt are taken away from us as we lay them at the cross.

Just as God forgives us, we have to forgive others and ourselves. When people hurt us, we can't hate them (or ourselves) but rather the sin that has been committed. Instead of condemning, we need to forgive, lay those sins at the cross, and pray for a heart of repentance for both ourselves and those who hurt us.

I want to pause here and help you to understand why God is so passionate about saving and healing His people. God loves His children with an incomprehensible love, but He hates the sins they commit. Sin not only severely injures our souls, but also it keeps us from knowing, believing, and trusting God, which deeply saddens Him (Isaiah 43:24). It also hurts our relationships with others.

Because God is holy, He can't tolerate sin. If we were to step into the presence of God, who is an all-consuming fire (Hebrews 12:29), we would immediately be consumed because all impurities are cremated by His fire. That is why Jesus had to come. Jesus had to die as a man because it was man that brought sin into the world. And the reason God predestined all men to be sinners once one man (Adam) sinned was so it would only take one man (Jesus) to atone for all people who place their faith in Him (Romans 5:17). Jesus is the atoning work of God's judgment against sin. Jesus—through His life, death, and resurrection—is the only way we can be justified and made righteous before God. When we place our faith in Jesus, God doesn't see our sin, He sees the blood of Jesus, and because of that, we are not consumed or separated from Him.

Besides eternal separation from God, sin also causes us pain and suffering. Just as physical pain reveals there is something wrong with our bodies, conviction is a warning or injured feeling that reveals we either have sin in our lives or are about to. This warning should lead us to God, for if it doesn't, we may end up condemning ourselves or others.

Being continually anxious or having a strong, inner, gloomy discomfort or dissatisfaction may be an indication that we are injured and in need of repentance. Proverbs 15:15 (AMP) talks about this: "All the days of the desponding and afflicted are made evil [by anxious thoughts and forebodings], but he who has a glad heart has a continual feast [regardless of circumstances]." Many times, these forebodings have a negative impact on our thoughts as well as our actions because we obsessively dwell and meditate on them. The only way to overcome these thoughts is by purposefully and radically replacing them with God's Word.

I lived with an anxious feeling for years, but instead of being convicted, I allowed fear to condemn me. If I felt someone didn't like me (no matter who it was), a foreboding of fear and condemnation would erupt within me. When I understood the truth of what I was feeling, I found the lie causing me to sin. The lie was that I am not good enough, which caused me to feel unworthy and inadequate, which then caused me to dwell on myself, which is sin (self-pity, self-reliance, self-focus—all prideful). Because I didn't understand the reality of redemption through Jesus Christ, I hung on tightly to the enemy's lies (condemnation). I even tried to overcome those feelings by being nicer to people or by avoiding them, but what I was doing was making myself a slave to an imperfect me.

Once I turned my condemnation into conviction, I began to lay those sins at the cross and focus more on God rather than myself. As I mentioned earlier, condemnation leads us to death and bondage; whereas, conviction leads us to the cross and freedom.

Diagnosing Sin through Prayer

Another way our sins are diagnosed is through prayer. Just like we would converse with our doctor concerning our diagnoses, we need to talk to God to see and know what is hurting us. You can ask: "Lord, why am I hurting?" "How can we get rid of this pain?" "What steps do I have to take to get better?" "What sin is hindering me from being the person You created me to be?" If we are not sure what sins are hurting us, we simply can ask God to show us.

Sometimes sin entangles us so much that it becomes who we are and we don't know any better. What we think, say, and do can all be reactions to the sin infecting us. Instead of understanding how far this sin has taken us away from God and from seeing the horrific effects it has on us, we continue to live in our injuries without even realizing it (probably because those we hang out with are doing the same thing). Unless God's light reveals it, we are clueless to the reality of our specific sins. In the previous chapter, we talked about how sin numbs our sensitivity toward God. We need His mirror to help us see those things that are weighing us down.

Diagnosing Sin through Testing

Being tested is another way our sins are diagnosed. As we are squeezed and poked, areas of tenderness will be exposed. The infected spots will be sensitive to pain and will cause us to respond negatively when those areas are irritated. If you have an infection of rebellion, you will not respond well when others make suggestions to you. When you have an infection of criticism, you will not respond positively to the genuine efforts of people.

We can observe ourselves to see if our responses produce death or life. If we negatively react to someone or something, we may have found an area of infection that needs healing. We should never forgo the fruit of the Spirit (love, joy, peace, patience, kindness, goodness, faithfulness, gentleness, and self-control) to "defend" ourselves. If we do, we need to ask God to shine His light of truth on our situation so we have complete understanding of why we are reacting in that manner.

The Israelites are a great example for us to understand what it means to be tested and to react negatively. They were tested for forty years, and for most of that time they complained, disobeyed, and refused to trust God. In Deuteronomy 8:2, Moses reminded them of those tests: "Remember how the LORD your God led you all the way in the desert these forty years, to humble you and to test you in order to know what was in your heart, whether or not you would keep his commands."

When the Israelites were delivered from slavery and led out of Egypt, they had the minds and hearts of slaves. God had to squeeze them and reveal to them what was in their hearts. There was no way they could be brought into the Promised Land as they were. What should have been a really quick trip ended up taking them forty years. God wanted them set apart as His people when they entered the Promised Land. If they had not been tested, tried, and made new, they eventually would have gone back to being slaves again once they were in the Promised Land. They would have conformed to the pagan world around them. God had to prepare them to be set apart. He did this by testing them, squeezing them, and revealing what was in their hearts. And through all of this He developed them into what His chosen nation needed to be.

Tests will reveal a lot of what is inside of us as we are squeezed and made uncomfortable. As the rottenness (sin) comes to light and is accurately diagnosed, we can then begin the process of treating our injuries by laying them at the cross.

Just as a doctor is pleased to help his patient, God is pleased when we are willing to see our injuries, because He then can lead us to His treatment plan. God wants us healed. He wants us to be saved and live as saved people. The question is: are you willing to be diagnosed?

Our Divine Surgeon

When I was pregnant with my second child, I was not expecting a complicated delivery. I had Justin almost three years earlier, so I knew exactly what to expect for Brandon's delivery (at least, I thought I did). During my labor, everything was going as planned until Brandon's heart rate dropped dramatically. The nurses immediately called my doctor to check on me. He knew right away something wasn't right and told the nurses to prep me for a cesarean. I was so scared. There were nurses everywhere, and I had no idea what was going on. I definitely wasn't prepared for what was about to transpire. All I could do was surrender and pray that my doctor knew what he was doing. I later learned that the umbilical cord had been wrapped around Brandon's neck. I was so grateful for my doctor that day. He saved my baby (and me).

Just as my doctor saved me physically, Jesus has saved me spiritually. Even though there are many surgeons who are qualified to save lives, Jesus is the only divine surgeon who can save us spiritually. There are no other surgeons out there who can do what Jesus can do—*none*.

God chose Jesus to save us. Check out these Old and New Testament verses that confirm this:

> Here is my servant, whom I uphold, my chosen one in whom I delight; I will put my Spirit on him and he will bring justice to the nations.
>
> —Isaiah 42:1

> In the beginning was the Word, and the Word was with God, and the Word was God. He was with God in the beginning. ... The Word became flesh.
>
> —John 1:1-2,14

Surely he took up our infirmities and carried our sorrows, yet we considered him stricken by God, smitten by him, and afflicted. But he was pierced for our transgressions, he was crushed for our iniquities; the punishment that brought us peace was upon him, and by his wounds we are healed.

—Isaiah 53:4–5

Just as the living Father sent me and I live because of the Father, so the one who feeds on me will live because of me.

—Jesus, according to John 6:57

Being Saved and Living Saved

We are not only saved by Jesus' wounds, but also we are healed by His wounds. The penalty for sin is eternal death—hell (Romans 6:23). To be delivered from this penalty, we must be redeemed and our sins atoned for. Knowing we're sinners in need of a Savior is a prerequisite for coming to Jesus. The more we know the specific sins infecting us, the clearer we will see our need.

Before Jesus came into my heart, I was uncomfortable with my lack of knowledge about Him. Not only did I not understand the reality of why I needed Jesus, but also my sins hindered me from wanting to know. Even my husband struggled with not wanting to know about Jesus at first. Jon's biggest obstacle was accepting Jesus as the only way to heaven. My biggest obstacle was seeing my need for a Savior. (I had based my salvation primarily on being a good person.)

There are many who wrestle with completely understanding salvation, but God is passionate in saving His people. He has not made salvation difficult for us. We don't have to work for it. All we have to do is believe what God has made known through the life, death, and resurrection of Jesus Christ and know with all our hearts that we need Him.

> For God so loved the world that he gave his one and only Son, that whoever believes in him shall not perish but have eternal life.
>
> —John 3:16

> If you confess with your mouth, "Jesus is Lord," and believe in your heart that God raised him from the dead, you will be saved.
>
> —Romans 10:9

Believing in Jesus has nothing to do with what you do and everything to do with accepting what He has done. Even though you may not know every sin infecting you, accepting Jesus as your high priest will cover all of your sins once and for all (Hebrews 7). Not only are you eternally saved when you believe in Jesus, but also you then can start living a saved life.

Have you been saved by Jesus? If not, stop right now and ask Him to come into your heart. You can even pray John 3:16 and Romans 10:9 (see above) or you can pray the prayer below to help you with this. This is the most important decision you will ever make.

> Jesus, please come into my heart. Forgive me of all my sins and help me to turn away from my old life by living more for You. I confess with my mouth You are Lord and I believe in my heart that God raised You from the dead. I receive You as my Savior and Lord of my life. In Your name I pray, Amen.

Being saved seems to be simple compared to what comes next: living saved. Being saved means we have found and accepted the qualified redemptive work of Jesus, who saves us from eternal death and separation from God. Living saved means we have surrendered to Him so we can be transformed into the likeness of Christ. In response, we then are able to live more for Him so others can be saved and transformed too. (God uses us as His hands and feet to the lost world.)

When I was first saved, I was still very infected with sin. Even though Jesus' blood eternally atoned for my sins, I was not healed from the infection caused by my sins. And because I was still wounded, I lived wounded (even though I was a believer). It was hard to do what God wanted me to do until I cooperated with His Spirit. As I began to let Jesus chisel out the cancer of sin, He began to heal those areas of infection with His truth. Again, this is why it is vital to feed on His Word—it is His truth that sets us free. The more I gave Jesus my sin, the more His Word had room to grow in me. And the more Jesus lived in me, the more His Spirit could lead me to what He wanted me to do. And that is what it means to live saved—Jesus becomes who you are.

Living saved is not about what we do; it's about who we are. Transformation starts with the inside and then naturally overflows to the outside. If we try to force our relationship with God by doing and working for Him instead of surrendering to Him, we will not only exhaust ourselves, but also we will never be transformed. The key factor to transformation is allowing God the opportunity to pour into us. We must first place ourselves where God's grace, His undeserving favor, can pour in and nourish us. This could be through prayer, church services, Sunday school, Bible studies, Christian books, talking with other Christians, or any other avenue where His Spirit is present.

Psalm 37:4 says, "Delight yourself in the LORD and he will give you the desires of your heart." When we delight in

God by placing ourselves in those places of God's grace, He will pour in and through us. Eventually, our desires will start to align with God's desires, and because we have delighted in Him, we will begin to want to do what He desires.

Have you been you saved? If so, are you living as though you have been saved? How will you begin to place yourself in His grace places?

The Operating Table

The operating table is not a place we would gladly choose to lie on. In fact, most of us would rather avoid it at all costs. But there are times when the operating table is our only option. The pain and suffering of our sicknesses cause us to grow completely weary and dependent—to a point of surrender. We finally realize, "I can't do this anymore, and I don't want to do this anymore." We step down from our throne of self and step up onto our Doctor's table—the place where our will and life melts in His hands. It is probably the most unsure place in our walk with God, but in the end, it is the most rewarding experience. Not only are we set free from being a slave to ourselves and what others think of us, but also we are radically liberated to start living as God intended us to, because we are made new in Him. Paul explained this process beautifully:

> Therefore, if anyone is in Christ, he is a new creation; the old has gone, the new has come! All this is from God, who reconciled us to himself through Christ and gave us the ministry of reconciliation: that God was reconciling the world to himself in Christ, not counting men's sins against them. And he has committed to us the message of reconciliation.
>
> —2 Corinthians 5:17–19

Here are a few verses that relate to the "operating table." Carefully read each one, and know that it is God's desire for these truths to become your reality.

He heals the brokenhearted and binds up their wounds.
—Psalm 147:3

Surely you desire truth in the inner parts; you teach me wisdom in the inmost place.
—Psalm 51:6

He sent forth his word and healed them; he rescued them from the grave.
—Psalm 107:20

And the God of all grace, who called you to his eternal glory in Christ, after you have suffered a little while, will himself restore you and make you strong, firm and steadfast.
—1 Peter 5:10

Happy and fortunate is the man whom God reproves; so do not despise or reject the correction of the Almighty [subjecting you to trial and suffering]. For He wounds, but He binds up; He smites, but His hands heal.
—Job 5:17–18 AMP

For we know that our old self was crucified with him so that the body of sin might be done away with, that we should no longer be slaves to sin—because anyone who had died has been freed from sin.
—Romans 6:6–7

Though you have made me see troubles, many and bitter, you will restore my life again; from the depths of the earth you will again bring me up.
—Psalm 71:20

The LORD will sustain him on his sickbed and restore him from his bed of illness. I said, "O LORD, have mercy on me; heal me, for I have sinned against you."

—Psalm 41:3–4

These verses are so powerful and have so much life in them. As we begin to lay ourselves on His table, these verses are the healing medicine to our souls. They have the power to heal our wounds as He digs out the infected cancer of sin. As each wound is being cleansed, His Word fills in where sin once was. Jesus, who is the Word, is necessary for our healing.

The Surgery Tools

My operating table experience was a confusing and disorienting ordeal. At the time, I didn't realize what the Lord was doing to me. I had no idea I was being "operated on" by God. I remember praying (right before He began to heal me) that God would show me who I was in Jesus Christ. Let me tell you something: I had no idea what my prayer meant from God's perspective. In the end, I acquired a new understanding of death and humility. To know who you are in Jesus requires a death before a resurrection, and it also requires humility before honor. Paul wrote it like this: "I want to know Christ and the power of his resurrection and the fellowship of sharing in his sufferings, becoming like him in his death, and so, somehow, to attain to the resurrection from the dead" (Philippians 3:10–11).

I also didn't know that God uses certain instruments to cut out our infectious sins. These tools are what shape us more into the image of His Son, Jesus. He chisels and chips away at those things in us that do not fit into the mold of Christ. God hand selected each instrument that was particular to me and my sins. I started noticing that the very thing that was infecting me was the very tool He used to heal me. He not only used my marriage as one of His tools, but also He used friends and different organizations and situations I was involved with.

One of the first infections God dug out of me was fear and self-reliance. God knew the perfect tool to use on me for this: fear itself. So what did God do? He called me to be a Bible study leader. Not only would I have to lead fifteen women for thirty-two weeks, but also I would have to face my fears—fear of failure and what people thought of me. I had such a cancer of people's opinions living inside of me, so He used leadership to dig that darkness out of me.

At the end of class each week, I felt like I left a piece of my flesh on the floor as I faced my fear of what my group thought of me as their leader. Even though my flesh did not like being worked on, God's Spirit gave me a peace and an assurance that I was exactly where I needed to be. Week after week as I stepped into my new role, God chiseled out my self-dependence and people's opinions and replaced them with confidence in and reliance on Him. I was becoming more like Him each week.

Another infection that crowded my soul was unhealthy expectations (of myself and others). Again, God knew the perfect tool to use for this: people who didn't seem to care for me. Growing up, I had always found my worth and value in the way people responded to me. If they ignored me or didn't say much to me, I thought something must be wrong with me. God wanted me to get over this in a *big* way, so He put people in my life who didn't pay me much attention. After being at one particular place, I would come home crying almost every week. I was trying so hard to fit in that I felt like a square peg trying to fit into a round hole. Yet, it seemed that the more I was ignored or undervalued, the harder I ran to God. Over time (and a lot of running to God), my broken heart and confusion turned into healing and clarity. God was using my "hurtful" situations to help me get over myself (and others) by teaching me how to put my worth and value in Him instead of in people.

At one point I kept hearing, *"Have no expectations—give me your expectations and the expectations others have on you."* As I began to depend on God instead of the law of expectations, He taught me that putting on and taking on expectations was dangerous. People's opinions were never meant to take the place of God's truth, and our opinions were never meant to be the truth we place on others. Our opinions and expectations, whether from ourselves or others, should always come from God. Sadly, this is not the case in the world we live in. Most people will judge others out of their own limited opinions and expectations instead of looking to see how God sees those particular people.

As believers, we should not let what others think of us discourage us. We have to purposefully focus on God's expectations. If we don't, we will become slaves to the expectations of ourselves and others.

Even though people's opinions can be a big infection to tackle, the big daddy to most of our sins is the infection of rebellion and pride. Turning pride into humility requires not only a big surgery tool but also a radical surrender on our part. Besides work and relationships, marriage is probably the greatest and most efficient tool God can use to help us get over ourselves. When we intimately live with someone year after year, we are given many opportunities to be transformed into Christ's image.

I was full of rebellion and pride. I didn't realize the extent of my pride until I started radically seeking God. I will be very honest with you; all of us are extremely prideful! Until we seriously surrender to God by seeking Him and soaking in His Word, we will never know God's definition of humility. Humility is not achieved by studying alone; it is achieved through experiencing sorrow and suffering. That is why James tells us to consider it pure joy whenever we face trials of many kinds (James 1:2).

God began to deal with my pride not only through my situations but also through my marriage. As I mentioned before, Jon and I had always been like best friends, but as soon as we started walking with God, we started having some major conflicts. We didn't understand what was happening to us at first, but later we came to realize that God was using that opposition to conform us and glue us together with His love. During this time, God was also working out our individual wounds that were causing our marriage harm.

I had to learn what it meant to respect my husband and to submit under his authority. If I was ever going to learn how to submit to God, I had to first learn how to submit to my husband. My pride was getting in the way of my fully submitting to Jon, but God slowly dug this out of me.

Even though Jon was not exactly where he needed to be, I still needed to submit. The Bible doesn't say to submit and respect your husband if … It says to submit to and respect your husband as unto the Lord. Submitting to and respecting your husband is an act of obedience unto the Lord. Let me just note that this does not mean we submit to or tolerate abusive behavior. Anyone who is being abused needs to seek not only God but also professional help immediately.

But for me, trying to submit to Jon was like trying to write with my left hand—it was awkward and my flesh did not like it. I would go through the motions, but my heart was not in it. There was a period when Jon would often call me or send me an email, asking me to do something for him. I even remember a couple of times when he typed out a list of things to do. At first, I would get so irritated by his interruptions. I would think, *Doesn't he realize I have my own duties and responsibilities? Why can't he do this himself? Why does he want this done anyway—we don't need to involve ourselves with this!* As this kept happening, I continually went to God to ask for forgiveness and for His Spirit to give me a heart to submit to Jon. It really bothered me that I felt this way toward Jon. I knew a wife was not to be irritated about helping her husband. As I told God my heart's desire, He showed me the delight of being my husband's helpmate and how my submission to Jon's requests actually showed Jon I cared for him.

I had to fight for my husband, because there was, and continues to be, a spiritual war going on over him that could hinder his leadership role for our family. I pictured myself holding Jon up through my submission, which drew Jon closer to God. I now look at myself as being a submission warrior for Jon. Through my submission, I am fighting for him, because the less rebellion I have, the more God can work though me to make an impact on his life. And the more God works in Jon's life, the more of an impact can be made for me and my children.

There are many instruments God can use—it just depends on what we need. He can use our trials, sufferings, difficulties, and aggravations. He can also use our situations, such as caring for an elderly parent or parenting a difficult child. Think about what you are going through right now, and ask God to help you use those things to conform you more into Christ's image. Instead of worrying or being frustrated, surrender to God and let Him use your situation to make you more beautiful. Having this kind of perspective with your trials will help you to make the most of them. First

Peter says, "Dear friends, do not be surprised at the painful trial you are suffering, as though something strange were happening to you. But rejoice that you participate in the sufferings of Christ, so that you may be overjoyed when his glory is revealed" (1 Peter 4:12–13).

The Surgery

Just like we all have physical bodies that often need healing, we all have souls that need healing as well. The soul is our mind, will, and emotions. When we experience an event that causes us stress or discouragement, our souls become targets for the Enemy. Traumas, frustrations, confusions, and temptations are the very things that make us weak, and the Enemy always knows when and where we are weak.

Every lie you believe becomes a wound on your soul. And, as we mentioned earlier, our wounds eventually manifest into sin if we don't heal them with God's Word. When our wounds are not dealt with, our minds, wills, and emotions will all react to the sins in our lives.

Here are just a few different indicators that your soul has been injured and infected with sin:

- Lashing out at others (verbally and physically)
- Hiding or withdrawing to avoid pain or disappointment
- Controlling or dominating someone who may seem weaker than you
- Exhibiting stubbornness and bitterness (you harbor resentment toward others)
- Exhibiting or expecting perfectionism (with yourself or with others)
- Causing strife (stirring up trouble in your relationships or circumstances)

- Busying yourself with activities and people for fulfillment
- Consuming yourself with addictions
- Judging or criticizing others
- Being overly fearful or passive
- Pacifying or being a catalyst for others' sins

It's hard to move forward and upward when we have these types of injuries holding us down. Instead of being nourished and controlled by the Holy Spirit, we muddle in our wounds. Paul explained it like this:

> Those who live according to the sinful nature have their minds set on what that nature desires; but those who live in accordance with the Spirit have their minds set on what the Spirit desires. The mind of sinful man is death, but the mind controlled by the Spirit is life and peace; the sinful mind is hostile to God. It does not submit to God's law, nor can it do so. Those controlled by the sinful nature cannot please God.
>
> —Romans 8:5–8

God desires for us to be healthy and strong, but without His light to reveal our wounds, we stay stuck in our injuries. Staying wounded keeps us in darkness and actually gives the Enemy an opening to torment us. We have no soundness because of our sin (Psalm 38:3). Unless we allow the Holy Spirit (who is perfect in Jesus Christ) to control us, we will continue to be controlled by our injured souls. As David said, "For the enemy has pursued and persecuted my soul, he has crushed my life down to the ground; he has made me to dwell in dark places as those who have been long dead" (Psalm 143:3 AMP).

Our souls need healing, and Jesus is the only One who can atone for, redeem, cut out, bind up, and dry out our injured souls. Just like a tumor being removed, when you lay a particular sin at the cross, that sin rooted in your soul is cut out. However, just because the sin is gone doesn't mean the wound is gone. Recognizing and laying our sins at the cross is only the first step. The wound left by sin now needs to be healed and replaced with God's Word. Once our injuries are filled and bound up with God's Word, the Enemy can then be loosened from us because he no longer has a right to torment us in that particular area that has been healed" (Matthew 16:19, 18:18).

Our wounds are healed by the working out of God's Word. As we begin to repent of our sins and study His truth, God will allow situations in our lives so that the Word gets into the cracks and crevices where sin once laid. "Continue to work out your salvation with fear and trembling, for it is God who works in you to will and to act according to his good purpose" (Philippians 2:12b–13). So don't be surprised when things start happening once you repent of your sins. God will work out your salvation by sanctifying you with His Word.

One reason we have such a hard time being set free is that our minds, wills, and emotions continue to dwell in the darkness of our wounds. A great example of this is found in Mark 5:2–8 (emphasis mine):

When Jesus got out of the boat, a man with an evil spirit came from the *tombs* to meet him. This man lived in the *tombs*, and no one could bind him any more, not even with a chain. For he had often been chained hand and foot, but he tore the chains apart and broke the irons on his feet. No one was strong enough to subdue him. Night and day among the *tombs* and in the hills he would cry out and cut himself with stones. When he saw Jesus from a distance, he ran and fell on his knees in front of him. He shouted at the top of his voice. "What do you want with me, Jesus, Son of the Most High God? Swear to God that you won't torture me!" For Jesus had said to him, "Come out of this man, you evil spirit!"

You may have noticed the word "tombs" repeated several times in this passage. The demon-possessed man lived and dwelled among the tombs. The word "tomb" carries with it the idea of recalling or remembering. It is a monument commemorating the dead. Oftentimes, we live and dwell among our own tombs of death—those events and people we remember and commemorate that wounded our souls. The longer we remember and dwell on those wounds, the longer we will live among the tombs.

Jesus has the power to deliver and cast out those deathly wounds that burden our souls. Jesus' death, the cross, is where we humbly place those wounds, and His resurrection is what makes it possible for our ashes to be turned into beauty. Just like a rainbow after a storm, our mourning can be transformed in gladness and our sorrow into joy (Jeremiah 31:13).

Soul Therapy

Often after surgery, there is a time of healing and physical therapy. Because our bodies have been dramatically altered by the doctor's scalpel, our flesh, tissue, muscles, blood vessels, and nerves also have been impacted. Even our thinking and emotions can be affected. So after surgery, there is usually a time of healing and restoration. Not only does our flesh start to heal, but also the wounds start to dry up and the body is restored. Where once we were not able to walk or lift an arm because of our injuries, now we can start to work on those areas that have been healed through surgery.

In the same way, when we allow our divine surgeon to scalpel our wounded souls, we will experience a phase during which those wounds will dry up and be restored. Where sin once lay, a dry desert is now waiting for His streams to flow:

> See, I am doing a new thing! Now it springs up; do you not perceive it? I am making a way in the desert and streams in the wasteland. The wild animals honor me, the jackals and the owls, because I provide water in the desert and streams in the wasteland, to give drink to my people, my chosen, the people I formed for myself that they may proclaim my praise.
>
> —Isaiah 43:19–21

Through repentance and reading God's Word, we have made a way for Him to quench our thirsty wastelands (where sin once consumed, God can now inhabit). Our soul is now able to incorporate and receive the living streams from the Holy Spirit. Jesus said, "Indeed, the water I give him will become in him a spring of water welling up to eternal life" (John 4:14). He also said, "Whoever believes in me, as the Scripture has said, streams of living water will flow from within him" (John 7:38). Through this restoration and transformation, we are able to proclaim praise to God for the work He has done in us.

As we become healed and restored, another aspect of our lives that has to be dealt with is our habits. When we are injured for a long period of time and then become healed, our ways of thinking and behaving will have to be healed too. For example, if you had a severely injured shoulder, over time you probably developed habits to compensate for that injury. But after surgery and physical therapy, your old way of doing things can be replaced with a new and restored way of doing things. However, this may be difficult because you were so accustomed to doing things the old, injured way. It may be scary to think you can now throw a football or a baseball. You may stay "injured" in your mind because you are so fearful of hurting yourself, but in reality, you are healed. Your body knows it can throw the ball, but your mind says you can't.

This is what happens to us when we are healed from our sins. Even though we may be healed, our old habits are hard to break, and we still wander in the tombs. If we are healed, we have to live and think healed. I remember at one point hearing, *"Laura, you are healed now. You can let go. Laura, you have to let go of the chains to lay hold of Me."*

At first, the hardest thing to let go of was my wrong thinking. I was so used to thinking in such a negative way that it was hard to process any other way. Like those forebodings we looked at earlier, I was still allowing my thoughts to hold me captive, even though I knew God's Word. But as I began to change my habits (especially my thoughts), my thinking became more focused on God. Now when I am around people, even though those anxious thoughts still come, I do my best to stand firm on His truth. I may feel the hit of the Enemy's arrows, but I immediately turn to God's Word to fight them off, thinking: *There is no condemnation for those who are in Jesus Christ. My worth and value do not come from the way people respond to me. I am not going to be perfect at everything. Everything God has made is good. I am not to be confident in myself but in God. Lean on God, and trust that He will use this for my good.*

Another unhealthy habit I had was the way I interpreted or heard things. For years, I listened with condemning ears. If someone, especially my husband, tried to correct or make a suggestion to me, I would take it personally, assuming that person was trying to condemn me. I would get defensive and irritated because those wounds taught me to be condemning with everything that came my way. As I began to heal, my old way of hearing started to change. Whenever I caught myself being defensive, the truth in me realized that my ears were hearing with condemnation, and I started to hear truthfully with God's ears.

The wounds, surgery, and even the therapy afterward can all be painful processes, but without the willingness to be healed, there is no freedom. It is up to you to choose what you are willing to surrender to: the wounds or the surgery that will lead to healing.

Finally Free

I love birds. I often will sit on my back patio for hours talking to God while I watch the birds fly on and off our bird feeders. Red cardinals are my favorite. They remind me of the blood Jesus shed for my sins. When I spend my mornings by my bedroom window praying, God will often send a red cardinal my way. I have shed many tears by that window, and it often seems like every time I need encouragement from God, a red cardinal will show up in my backyard. I just know it is God's way of assuring me that He hears me and is with me. God also teaches me that despite my sins, Jesus' blood covers me and His grace sets me free, just like those red cardinals are free to fly.

We too can have wings to fly above the thoughts and circumstances that often hurt us. We can see beyond our doubts and confusion that cloud our vision. We can have the blood of Jesus protecting us from being trapped in sin caused by lies. When we have been healed and set free, our sins don't have to keep us stuck in a web of lies. We are able to fly high above the world around us and see things from an aerial view—the way God sees things. We are able to fix our eyes not on what is seen but on what is unseen because we know that "what is seen is temporary and what is unseen is eternal" (2 Corinthians 4:18).

Being healed enables us to have the strength and assurance of freedom in Jesus Christ. Freedom is nothing we can force to happen—it is the result of being healed. When the Holy Spirit is free to flow within us (because our wounds have been healed), we can't help but be free. Through this freedom, we will have a strong and uncontrollable desire to live for Christ. We become like Jesus because it is His Spirit filling us and enabling us to love others. Instead of being controlled by our feelings, emotions, and what others think, we are controlled by His Spirit.

The perfect demonstration of true freedom is when Jesus lived on earth as a man. He walked in freedom because he was always in perfect union with His Father. From a worldly view, Jesus didn't seem like much: " … he had no beauty or majesty to attract us to him" (Isaiah 53:2). He had "no place to lay his head" (Luke 9:58). He was not an earthly king or rich, and He wasn't worried about appearance or status. He was hated without reason (John 15:25). And in the end, He was "despised and rejected by men" and was "crushed for our iniquities" (Isaiah 53:3–5). But with all that, Jesus was still glad to do the Father's will. Jesus was actually satisfied to do the Father's will (Isaiah 53:11). That is because He did not live for Himself but for His Father. Jesus said, "I tell you the truth, the Son can do nothing by himself; he can do only what he sees his Father doing because whatever the Father does the Son also does" (John 5:19).

True freedom is to live for Christ. When we let go of the throne to self and lay hold of Him, we relinquish our lives to Him. Instead of living out our desires, we live out

God's desires. We are now no longer slaves to ourselves but servants to Jesus Christ. "For a man is a slave to whatever has mastered him" (2 Peter 2:19). That is how you know when you are truly free—you live for Jesus.

Whom do you live more for—yourself or Jesus?

CHAPTER 7

Truly Beautiful

Ordinary to Extraordinarily Beautiful

BEFORE I WAS transformed and started seeing things through the eyes of the Holy Spirit, my recognition of the Lord's extraordinary beauty was veiled. Day after day and year after year, I would pass up or disregard the wonderful treasures He had spread before me. I categorized those extraordinary opportunities and labeled them as ordinary. Instead of embracing what God had for me, I went my own way and looked to what I thought was exciting or worth my time. But as His Spirit began to grow in me, those ordinary things blossomed into an array of divine elegance right before my eyes. And it seemed that the more I could see His elaborate grace, the more I was filled with His beautiful joy and divine peace.

Because of my new insights, I began to humbly praise God not only for my salvation in Him but also for each day He gave me. I realized and took to heart that each day was a gift from God wrapped in an ornate bow of grace.

Lamentations states, "Because of the LORD's great love we are not consumed, for his compassions never fail. They are new every morning; great is your faithfulness (Lamentations 3:22–23). Like this verse says, God's mercies and grace are new every day, and because of that, I can enjoy and be blessed by the many provisions He gives me each day: His sun and moon, His colors and textures, His rain and air, His trees and flowers, His birds and butterflies, and His beautiful children (just to name a few). I also enjoy the incredible privileges and freedoms I have in this country, the provision of my husband's job, and the schools my children attend. It is because of God that I am able to have such treasures. Yes, my husband and I may work hard and pay taxes, but everything we have is from God—even our talents and abilities. And for that we are grateful. Because I used to take these wonderful gifts for granted, I was never able to treasure or really value God's gifts.

I was blinded by the darkness of lies in my earlier years, so I overlooked and missed out on seeing not only the splendor of God but also my own inner beauty. But as I began to let God chip away at my hardened heart, He began to give me a heart of flesh (Ezekiel 11:19), and it was only then that my ordinary and ungrateful view of life started to turn into an incredible appreciation of what God has placed in and all around me. Through all of this, I have come to learn and embrace that it is not what we see with our eyes that matters most but more how we see with our hearts. Our hearts make us see, and if we have hearts of stone, we will see most things as ordinary and unimportant. But if we have hearts of flesh, we will see the way God sees—extraordinarily and beautifully.

Jesus is a perfect example of how we can easily overlook God's divine beauty. Many people saw and continue to see Jesus as ordinary. This is because they saw and continue to see Him with their eyes instead of with their hearts. But one day very soon, everyone will come to see Jesus as He really is, and when they do, every knee will bow (Isaiah 45:23; Romans 14:11; Philippians 2:10). Instead of coming back as the little baby born in Bethlehem, Jesus will come back as Lord of Lords and King of Kings (see Revelation 19:11–16)!

As a man, Jesus knew He couldn't attract the common eye to Him in a worldly and materialistic way. In fact, only those God drew to Jesus would be attracted to Him. Jesus had to go to the cross. He had to be broken so we could be healed. And because most people tend to be drawn to the shallowness of appearance and secular popularity, like we tend to be with celebrities today, Jesus was overlooked and rejected by the majority of those around Him. But Jesus did not waiver because of what others thought of Him. He stood firm on what God had sent Him to do. Jesus knew He was not in the world to live it up as an earthly king but rather to die so others could be saved from being eternally separated from God. In His own words:

> The hour has come for the Son of Man to be glorified. I tell you the truth, unless a kernel of wheat falls to the ground and dies, it remains only a single seed. But if it dies, it produces many seeds. The man who loves his life will lose it, while the man who hates his life in this world will keep it for eternal life. Whoever serves me must follow me; and where I am, my servant also will be. My Father will honor the one who serves me. Now my heart is troubled, and what shall I say? "Father, save me from this hour"? No, it was for this very reason I came to this hour. Father, glorify your name!
>
> —John 12:23–28

Jesus' life is such an example for us. He taught us that through death, life is given. Because of Him, when we die to ourselves, we are making room for Jesus to live in us. And that is what it means to be beautiful.

> Your beauty should not come from outward adornment, such as braided hair and the wearing of gold jewelry and fine clothes. Instead, it should be that of your inner self, the unfading beauty of a gently and quiet spirit, which is of great worth in God's sight. For this is the way the holy women of the past *who put their hope in God used to make themselves beautiful.*
> —1 Peter 3:3–5, emphasis added

Being beautiful is more about who we are on the inside than what we wear and what we do on the outside. It is more about glorifying God than it is about glorifying ourselves. Sometimes our outward appearances and actions do not match the inward reality of our hearts. True beauty starts from the inside and works its way outward. It is not something we can force to happen. It is something that occurs when we surrender to God. The more radically we let God deal with us, the more extraordinarily beautiful we will become.

I remember for years trying to be beautiful in the eyes of others. At the time, my definition of beauty was not just what I looked like; it was more about being relationally connected with others. One of the reasons I felt ugly was because people didn't seem to be drawn to me. When I would cautiously open my heart to others, most of them did not have the same desire to befriend me on the same level. I felt so awkward when this happened because it just didn't make sense to me. It seemed like the harder I tried, the worse things got and the more isolated I became. I just wanted to connect with people, but for some reason, I only connected with a few (which I now realize is not a bad thing).

As the years progressed, my fear of rejection grew and my image became more and more distorted. It wasn't until I willingly surrendered to God that I realized my approach to beauty was not God's approach. It wasn't about connecting with people; it was more about connecting with God. Instead of looking at God to define me, I looked at myself and others to define me. However, God did not leave me alone, and He allowed me to get into situations that would draw me to Him as I started looking for answers.

God used one friendship in particular to help me realize that people could never uphold the satisfaction and connection that only He could. This person was someone I desperately wanted to be friends with, but her idea of friendship was different than mine. She liked being with groups of people and enjoyed more of a social environment. She was fun, upbeat, popular, and very nice. Yet, the one thing I really struggled with was the one-sidedness of this friendship. Even though she listened to me and was always nice to me, she rarely opened her heart to me. I started to feel like the desperate friend who needed her more than she needed me. At the time, I desired a more intimate, less casual friendship—where both parties equally shared their hurts and feelings with each other. Even though there was nothing wrong with either of our "friendship styles," it was not the compatible connection I had expected. We were at different places in our lives, but God used those differences to help me find myself in Him.

Through these types of struggles, God started teaching me and transforming me into His image. As I began to focus less on others, He slowly began to draw people to me, which meant I wasn't working hard to draw myself to people. I am now learning how to be more content with myself (whether alone or with others) because I am learning to appreciate who I am in Jesus, for it is He who makes me beautiful.

What relationships are you struggling with? Who may God be using in your life to draw you to Him?

Living Beautifully in the Fruit and Light of His Resurrection

Even though the cross was the end of sin and death, the resurrection was the beginning of all things beautiful. Jesus' resurrection bestows on us a "crown of beauty instead of ashes" (Isaiah 61:3). Because Jesus rose on the third day, there is resurrection hope for all of us who place our faith in Him. But before we can start living in the beauty of the resurrection, we have to place all things that make us ugly at the cross. The cross is where we hang our sin, shame, hurt, confusion, inadequacies, insecurities, fears, guilt, rejection, worries, and doubts. The cross is the dumping ground for every sin and lie that has set itself against God. As you stand in front of God's mirror and allow Him to reveal your hurts and sins, place everything He exposes at the cross. Confess it and lay it down daily—not out of guilt but out of a desperate need to be set free.

Many times we get so caught up in the little things that we miss the big picture of what it really means to be set free. We think that once we start having a relationship with God, we have to live bound by a bunch of rules. Remember, God doesn't need anything from us—He is the one who saves and helps us. Having a relationship with God is more of a heart condition than it is about a checklist of things to give up.

First, God wants us to see and know with all of our hearts how much we need Him. As we surrender to that need, He begins to reveal those things that are harming our relationship with Him. If we try to give up our old habits with unchanged hearts, we will eventually go back to our old ways.

We don't need to follow a list of rules, we need to follow Jesus. So stop dwelling on the "rules," and start pursuing Jesus. The more we go after Him, the more of a disciplined desire *Jesus will give us* to turn away from those things that are hurting us. We can never change in our own strength, nor should we desire to—that would become legalism. Jesus has to give us that desire to want to change. Don't let the Enemy tell you that living a life with God is about "giving up" things. It is more about letting God change your heart so you can begin to let go of the old and take on the better things He has for you.

There are four S.A.F.E ways in which we can follow Jesus to accomplish this:

- Surrender to Jesus' power.
- Acknowledge His presence (hourly).
- Formal prayer (daily).
- Expect and believe God will help you.

First, when we surrender to the vine power of Jesus, our branches will be strong and productive. In John 15:5–8, we learn that Jesus is the vine, and as believers, we are the branches. When we remain in Christ, we will bear much fruit (for apart from Him we can do nothing). Just as the vine is the source of all fruit, Jesus is the source of our harvest. The only way a branch bears fruit is if the vine produces it. The branch is weak and useless without the vine, but attached to the vine, we branches hold and display the fruit Jesus produces. The best way to abide in Christ is through His Word and prayer.

Second, when we acknowledge Jesus throughout each day, our thoughts will be aligned with His. We are to "be joyful always; pray continually; give thanks in all circumstances" (1 Thessalonians 5:16–18). Because our flesh and the world around us are always nagging us, we have to constantly remember and purposefully think about Jesus—if not every minute, at least every hour of each day. This is the only way to align our ordinary and foul thoughts to the extraordinary and beautiful Word of Jesus (2 Corinthians 10:5).

Third, formally praying to God each day is something we can't neglect if we want to keep in step with Jesus. Making a daily appointment with God is crucial in a chaotic and busy world. God is the *only* constant in our lives. When everything around us seems unstable or unsure, we can know for sure that God is stable. He is the perfect in an imperfect world.

Not only is daily prayer an opportunity to praise God and make our requests known to Him, but also it is how we learn to hear from Him. If you don't know how to pray to God, start off by just talking to Him (like you would with a friend) for ten minutes every morning. Even though you may feel awkward at first, watch and wait patiently as God begins to respond to your prayers. He wants to reveal Himself to you.

Fourth, if we have surrendered to Jesus and have gone to Him in prayer, we should expect that God will help us. This expectation enables us to be confident and firm in our faith. Scripture says, "Wait and hope for and expect the Lord; be brave and of good courage and let your heart be stout and enduring. Yes, wait for and hope for and expect the Lord" (Psalm 27:14 AMP).

If for some reason you feel God isn't answering your prayers, ask Him for wisdom. He may be trying to work something out in you first, or He may be teaching you how to trust in Him with endurance and patience. Just because you don't see results doesn't mean your prayer hasn't been answered. God is very patient and long-suffering. As Isaiah says, "Yet the LORD longs to be gracious to you; he rises to show you compassion. For the LORD is a God of justice. Blessed are all who wait for him!" (Isaiah 30:18).

Following Jesus can be difficult at first. Many times we lack the desire and patience to follow Him. It is no fun trying to do something we don't want to do. So how do we deal with these feelings? John Piper's practical but profound teaching in his book *The Dangerous Duty of Delight*[6] may help you with this dilemma:

> I am often asked what a Christian should do if the cheerfulness of obedience is not there. It's a good question. My answer is not to simply get on with your duty because feelings don't matter. They do! My answer has three steps. First, confess the sin of joylessness. ("My heart is faint; lead me to the rock that is higher than I," Psalm 61:2.) Acknowledge the coldness of your heart. Don't say that it doesn't matter how you feel. Second, pray earnestly that God would restore the joy of obedience. ("I delight to do Your will, O my God; Your Law is within my heart," Psalm 40:8.) Third, go ahead and do the outward dimension of your duty in the hope that the doing will rekindle the delight.

From my own personal experience, these steps do work. There have been times when I felt like there was a war going on inside of me. My flesh kicked and screamed, but the Holy Spirit was humbly directing and nudging me. Deep within, I didn't want to settle for those selfish feelings—so I broke down and realized that if I didn't give my mess to the Lord, I would become a slave to it. So I brought my junk to the cross and asked God to give me a joyful and strong heart to do what I knew He wanted me to do. A broken heart is so beautiful to God. "The sacrifices of God are a broken spirit; a broken and contrite heart, O God, you will not despise" (Psalm 51:17).

Just like bearing fruit, living in the light of His resurrection means shining His light on those around us, just like a lamp brightens a room. We do this by plugging into and abiding in Jesus. Relying on ourselves and others is a temporal and weak outlet with no eternal value. And plugging into church once a week will only bring a limited amount of the power supply we need to shine brightly.

Imagine having a lamp that only illuminated for a couple of hours on Sunday, and the rest of the week, it didn't work. It would be impossible to live very effectively as we tried to find our way around. In the same way, we can't be beautiful in the way God intended if we are walking in the darkness of our own wisdom six days a week.

To effectively shine, we can't just hear about God's truths; we also have to believe them. Even though faith starts with hearing, it only penetrates when we believe what we hear. His Word must go from our ears to our minds to our hearts and, ultimately, to our feet. Our feet are just the caboose to the train of what fills our minds and hearts. We can make a list of what we do each day, and that will be a good indicator of what is controlling us. Even if we work or go to school or take care of our families, how we handle our responsibilities is a testimony of who we are. Are we guided by God, or are we guided by our own wisdom and insight? Is His light shining to those around us?

When I became a leader for my Bible study, I was filled with feelings of inadequacy. It was hard to trust in God because I had trusted in myself for most of my life. But I learned through Bible study that God isn't looking for adequate people. He is looking for those who will put their trust and faith in Him. I also learned that God chooses the foolish to shame the wise.

> God chose the foolish things of the world to shame the wise; God chose the weak things of the world to shame the strong. He chose the lowly things of this world and the despised things—and the things that are not—to nullify the things that are, so that no one may boast before him.
>
> —1 Corinthians 1:27–29

I was so surprised that God would pick someone like me to do something for Him. But I learned that it was more than just doing something for Him. Stepping into leadership was going to do something for me. It was going to teach me how to trust in God and how to get over myself. It was also going to teach me that God's grace is sufficient for me and His power is made perfect in my weakness (2 Corinthians 12:8).

I couldn't just hear these words. I had to believe and do them. I had to give God my weaknesses so He could prove His strength through them. I had to trust that even though the world may see me as foolish, God does not. And this is how God's light started shining through me. I had to not only hear Him, but also I had to believe and do what He said. The Bible says, "Do not merely listen to the word, and so deceive yourselves. Do what it says" (James 1:22).

When we hear His Word, God will give us opportunities to put His Word into action. Just as students are tested on what they learn, God's children are tested on what He teaches. It is not so much to prove that we know God. It is more about fully absorbing what we have learned. His truths have to be worked out. God drew me to Bible study before He called me to be a Bible study leader. In His perfect timing, He then tested me by calling me into leadership. It was through leadership that His Word became a reality in my life as I stepped out in faith.

Once His Word is flowing through our minds and hearts, it starts to penetrate our darkness as we put into action what we have learned. Then His light fills in those gaps where sin once lay. Not only do we start shining, but also we start moving. And that is how His Word is a lamp to our feet and a light for our path (Psalm 119:105). It really is a beautiful thing: "How beautiful on the mountains are the feet of those who bring good news, who proclaim peace, who bring good tidings, who proclaim salvation, who say to Zion, 'Your God reigns!'" (Isaiah 52:7; Romans 10:15).

Beautifully Fit to Run the Race

In Chapter 1 we talked about the journey to truth and how to get on God's eternal path for our lives. We also learned in later chapters that once we start following Jesus, He begins to work out those things that hurt us so we can be beautifully fit to run the race He has set out for us. What Jesus begins, He always completes. "He Who began a good work in you will continue until the day of Jesus Christ [right up to the time of His return], developing [that good work] and perfecting and bringing it to full completion in you" (Philippians 1:6 AMP).

When Jesus is your spiritual fitness trainer, He will perfect His good work in you to completion. You don't have to worry about if you are fit or if you are doing the right "workout." Jesus will instruct you step-by-step in exactly what exercise you need. You just have to patiently and fervently follow His unique workout routine, which always starts by feeding on His truths.

The apostle Paul not only explained how to train for and run the race but also where our focus needs to be as we are running:

> Do you not know that in a race all the runners run, but only one gets the prize? Run in such a way as to get the prize. Everyone who competes in the games goes into strict training. They do it to get a crown that will not last; but we do it to get a crown that will last forever. Therefore I do not run like a man running aimlessly; I do not fight like a man beating the air. No, I beat my body and make it my slave so that after I have preached to others, I myself will not be disqualified for the prize.
> —1 Corinthians 9:24–27

It is inspiring to hear how passionate Paul was for Jesus. He was so committed to living His life for Christ. His feet were so committed to proclaiming the good news. He "beat his body" by denying himself and dying to his own sinful nature so that he could stay healthy to preach the good news and receive the prize after the eternal finish line. Paul knew that those who glorify God and serve the Lord wholeheartedly will be rewarded for all the good they do (Ephesians 6:7–8).

Even though Paul was extraordinarily fit to run the race, he was not that way in the beginning. Before Paul met Jesus on the road to Damascus, he was called Saul and was very unfit to run any kind of race for the Lord. In fact, he was running away from and against God by persecuting Christians. Paul's story is a great example of what it looks like to go from running against God to running for God:

> Saul was still breathing out murderous threats against the Lord's disciples. He went to the high priest and asked him for letters to the synagogues in Damascus, so that if he

found any there who belonged to the Way, whether men or women, he might take them as prisoners to Jerusalem. As he neared Damascus on his journey, suddenly a light from heaven flashed around him. He fell to the ground and heard a voice say to him, "Saul, Saul, why do you persecute me?" "Who are you, Lord?" Saul asked. "I am Jesus, whom you are persecuting," he replied. "Now get up and go into the city, and you will be told what you must do." The men traveling with Saul stood there speechless; they heard the sound but did not see anyone. Saul got up from the ground, but when he opened his eyes he could see nothing. So they led him by the hand into Damascus. For three days he was blind, and did not eat or drink anything.

—Acts 9:1–9

Jesus met Paul where he was and turned him away from his destructive life of rebellion to living for Christ. Jesus had a purpose for Paul, and it wasn't to persecute Christians. Paul was going to be the one God used to preach the good news to the Gentiles. Yet, before Paul could do anything for God's kingdom, he had to be put on God's divine path and made fit for the work Christ had set out for him. Notice that Jesus blinded Paul for three days. Sometimes Jesus will halt us in the middle of our destructive path so He can get our attention and redirect us to His path.

Jesus is passionately committed to taking care of His sheep—even those who are wandering aimlessly and destructively. No sin is ever too big for Jesus.

Paul's conversion gave him the passion to run hard for Christ. He knew how low his rebellion had taken him, but he also knew "where sin increased, grace increased all the more" (Romans 5:20). God's grace of forgiveness had covered the lowest of Paul's sins, and because of that, he had been powerfully transformed. God's grace of forgiveness is what gave Paul the relentless passion to help others who were just as lost as he once was.

Paul said near the end of his life, "I have fought the good fight, I have finished the race, I have kept the faith" (2 Timothy 4:7). Can you say the same? Are you willing to be trained to run the race? Are you running hard for God's kingdom?

Little Steps Lead to Bigger Steps

As we begin to let Jesus train us and as we begin to run the race, our training will be based on the particular methods Jesus uses for each unique person. None of us will train and run exactly the way Paul did, and you won't train or run like I do. Each of us has a very specific call on our life that nobody else can mirror. That is why it is so important to look only at God as your main trainer and mentor. He is the One who made you in the particular ways that are specific to you. His plans for you are perfectly created to fit you and only you. He customizes everything and makes each person and plan in unique ways.

Many times we want to be like the apostle Paul or Billy Graham, but our personalities and circumstances may be nothing like theirs. I can't force myself to be like Paul. I could try, but in the end, I would be miserable and would not glorify God. I would be looking to Paul rather than looking to God. Now don't get me wrong; it is good to look up to people as examples, but they should never become God's replacements. God doesn't want us to compare ourselves (so stop comparing); instead, He wants us to find out who we are in Him. We are the clay; He is the potter.

Just like a baby or a ball of clay, we all have to start somewhere. Some of us may have been sixty years old and well-educated when we received Jesus into our hearts; but some of us may have been eight years old and in an abusive home when we became believers. Either way, we all have to give ourselves to Christ before we can be fit to run. Then, once we start running, we will have to run race after race after race. The first race may be more training than actually running for God's kingdom. The key is to grow persistently and progressively stronger with each step.

We must never neglect the areas God has already trained us in. For example, we wouldn't sign up for a second marathon and neglect a healthy workout routine and diet. Those are the basics of our initial training. We should be moving into a more disciplined and structured training that teaches us about endurance and stamina. When we neglect the basics of what we have already been trained for, that is a good indicator that we are backsliding. Even when we are idle, we eventually will start backsliding. We should always be growing but never neglecting what has already been set in place.

And sometimes we can be so focused on where we want to be that we neglect where we are. Instead of worrying about where you want to be, focus more on where you are now, and look to God to show you how you can take small, but ever-increasing steps toward Him.

God isn't going to give you something big like a worldwide ministry if you still have dirty dishes in the sink. Basically, if we can't handle the small things, how can we be equipped to handle the big things? Remember, God never gives us more than we can handle. So He starts us out small, and as we pass each test (or responsibility), He moves us onto the next step. Paul explained it like this:

> Brothers, I could not address you as spiritual but as worldly—mere infants in Christ. I gave you milk, not solid food, for you were not yet ready for it. Indeed, you

are still not ready. You are still worldly. For since there is jealousy and quarreling among you, are you not worldly? Are you not acting like mere men?

—1 Corinthians 3:1–3

Paul is saying that our actions will determine whether we are growing or still acting like infants. To grow and be set apart for God's kingdom means we live differently, more like Jesus. Once we start feeding on His milk and grow accordingly, He will give us solid food, along with bigger opportunities. The key is to feed and grow up ... feed and grow up ... feed and grow up.

Are you feeding on His truths? How are you growing stronger and becoming more beautiful?

Protecting Your Beauty

There are millions if not billions of dollars spent each year on beauty-related products. Not only do we spend lots of money, but also we spend lots of time and energy on our beauty by going to doctors, shopping, reading, worrying, and making ourselves up each day. Being attractive is an investment, but lately it seems to be losing its value as we realize that being pretty can't sustain or satisfy us.

I would say the most important beauty decision we could ever make besides receiving Jesus as our personal Savior is to study God's Word and pray to Him every day. These are the greatest treasures in the entire universe. This is what God says about these treasures:

My son, if you accept my words and store up my commands within you, turning your ear to wisdom and applying your heart to understanding, and if you call out for insight and cry aloud for understanding, and if you look for it as for silver and search for it as for hidden

treasure, then you will understand the fear of the Lord and find the knowledge of God.
—Proverbs 2:1–5

Blessed is the man who finds wisdom, the man who gains understanding, for she is more profitable than silver and yields better returns than gold. She is more precious than rubies; nothing you desire can compare with her.
—Proverbs 3:13–15

My purpose is that they may be encouraged in heart and united in love, so that they may have the full riches of complete understanding, in order that they may know the mystery of God, namely, Christ, in whom are hidden all the treasures of wisdom and knowledge.
—Colossians 2:2–3

Until we are with Jesus in heaven, we will need to protect our beauty from sin. As our wounds caused from sin begin to heal, our adversary will attempt to attack us; he will not leave us alone without a fight. He knows that once we are healed and walking in truth, he no longer has dominion over us in those areas where sin once dwelled. And even then, he may try to reopen those wounds. Jesus explained it like this:

When an evil spirit comes out of a man, it goes through arid places seeking rest and does not find it. Then it says, "I will return to the house I left." When it arrives, it finds the house unoccupied, swept clean and put in order. Then it goes and takes with it seven other spirits more wicked than itself, and they go in and live there. And the final condition of that man is worse than the first. That is how it will be with this wicked generation.
—Matthew 12:43–45

That is why it is so important that when you repent those wounds caused by sin are replaced with God's truth. If not, your house will remain empty, and the Enemy will know it and come back with even more vengeance. We may be reformed, but if we lack God's presence and power, our house is left open to be reoccupied by evil. We have to replace our sins with God's truth and protect ourselves from the Enemy's attacks. The Enemy has no power over Jesus, who is the Word (John 1:1–2), so feeding on and praying God's Word is how we protect ourselves.

It is also important to surround ourselves with other believers. We will need their support and nourishment. (We are stronger in unity than we are alone.) If we have a friend who is not building us up, we may not want to invest a lot of time with that person, unless God is calling us to minister to him or her. There are some great verses about who to pick for your friends:

A friend loves at all times.
—Proverbs 17:17

A man of many companions may come to ruin, but there is a friend who sticks closer than a brother.
—Proverbs 18:24

Therefore, since we are surrounded by such a great cloud of witnesses, let us throw off everything that hinders and the sin that so easily entangles, and let us run with perseverance the race marked out for us.
—Hebrews 12:1

Wounds from a friend can be trusted, but an enemy multiplies kisses.
—Proverbs 27:6

> You adulterous people, don't you know that friendship with the world is hatred toward God? Anyone who chooses to be a friend of the world becomes an enemy of God.
>
> —James 4:4

Next to investing wisely in our time with God, investing wisely in who we associate with can be just as important. Friends who build us up will encourage us to be and nourish us so we can be the person God desires us to be—those kind of friends give us the desire to run hard after God. But a friend who encourages us to sin is one who "multiplies kisses" (Proverbs 27:6). A true friend will point us away from those things that harm us, even though we may not like what he or she says (our pride doesn't like to be told we are doing wrong).

True beauty can't be bought, and it can't be bargained for. It already has been paid for in full by Jesus. Beauty is His gift to us; we just have to be willing to put it on. As a little girl who tried to buy her beauty through perfectionism and self-righteousness, I have traded those ashes for His beauty. I now live in the freedom of what He has already done for me. By His wounds I have been healed. I am now a diamond in His crown. My mourning has been covered with His anointing oil of gladness. My despair has been replaced with a garment of praise. He calls me an oak of righteousness, a planting of the Lord for the display of His splendor. He rebuilt and restored me. Instead of shame, I am receiving a double portion. Instead of disgrace, I am rejoicing in His inheritance. Everlasting joy is mine because I delight in Jesus, for He has clothed me with His salvation and robed me in His righteousness. Just as a bride who adorns herself with jewels, I am now a crown of splendor in the Lord's hand, a royal diadem in the hand of my God.

No longer am I called deserted or desolate. Instead, God had delighted in me and He rejoices in me—not in what I have done, but in what He has done in me. He has made me beautiful in Jesus (See Isaiah 61)!

You too can be beautiful! It is not only God's will to adorn you with His riches, but also it is His desire and delight. God has everything prepared and ready to give to you—all you have to do is willingly peel off your old rags of self-righteousness and put on His robe of righteousness. God has made *everything* available to us to overcome not only our flesh but also the world.

> I have told you these things, so that in Me you may have [perfect] peace and confidence. In the world you have tribulation and trials and distress and frustration; but be of good cheer [take courage; be confident, certain, undaunted]! For I have overcome the world. [I have deprived it of power to harm you and have conquered it for you.]
>
> —John 16:33 AMP

So I have to ask: Are you ready to see yourself in the mirror of truth? Are you ready and willing to let God do His thing with you so He can display His splendor through you? It is my prayer and expectation that His truth will indeed set you free to be truly beautiful in Jesus Christ.

Endnotes

1. Wikipedia, "compass," http://en.wikipedia.org/wiki/Compass.
2. Platt, David, *Radical*, (Multnomah Books, 2010), 179.
3. Evans, Tony, *The Battle is the Lord's*, (Moody Publishers, 1998), 47-49.
4. Evans, Tony, *The Kingdom Agenda*, (Moody Publishers, 1999,2006), 48.
5. Mittelberg, Mark, *Choosing Your Faith In a World of Spiritual Options*, (Tyndale House Publishers, 2008), Back Cover.
6. Piper, John, *The Dangerous Duty of Delight*, (Multnomah Publishers, 2001), 30-31.